365
Meditations
for Busy People

365
Meditations
for Busy People

Magpie Books, London

Constable & Robinson Ltd
3 The Lanchesters
162 Fulham Palace Road
London W6 9ER
www.constablerobinson.com

This edition published by Magpie Books,
an imprint of Constable & Robinson Ltd 2005

ISBN 1 84529 195 6

A copy of the British Library Cataloguing in
Publications Data is available from the British Library

Printed and bound in the EU

1

Release your stress and worries

1. Get into a comfortable position and close your eyes.
2. Take three deep breaths.
3. Visualize all the stress in your mind and body as a cloud of gray smoke. Allow this cloud to be released through the crown of your head. Imagine the gray cloud floating into the sky and disappearing. Feel the weight of the stress being released out of your body and into the cloud. Allow your shoulders to drop and continue until you have no more gray smoke, or for about ten minutes.

2

A calming mantra exercise

As you sit in your meditation position mentally go through the following checklist as you deepen your breathing:

* My thighs are relaxed.
* My feet are relaxed.
* My calves are relaxed.
* My buttocks are relaxed.
* My hands are relaxed.
* My arms are relaxed.
* My abdomen is relaxed.
* My chest is relaxed.
* My back is relaxed.
* My shoulders are relaxed.
* My neck is relaxed.
* My face and jaw are relaxed.
* My eyes are relaxed.
* My temples and forehead are relaxed.
* My scalp is relaxed.
* My head is relaxed.
* I am relaxed.

3

Steps to make meditation more effective

❖ You must have the desire to make a positive change in your life.

❖ You must believe in the power of the mind.

❖ You must accept the process of meditation including the results.

❖ Decide on what you want and be committed to it.

❖ Create the vision in your imagination and make it clear.

❖ Focus on it often, keep the images of your goal in your mind as often as possible.

❖ Keep your frame of mind and thoughts positive.

4

Clear your mind and concentrate solely on the one thought that concerns you. When you make your mind stick to one thought, it becomes stilled and your energy is conserved. Your problems become easier to manage.

5

If there is to be peace in the world,
There must be peace in the nations.
If there is to be peace in the nations,
There must be peace in the cities.
If there is to be peace in the cities,
There must be peace between neighbors.
If there is to be peace between neighbors,
There must be peace in the home.
If there is to be peace in the home,
There must be peace in the heart.

Lao Tse, 6th century BC

6

When you first try to meditate a lot of
thoughts will crowd your mind. Try to put all
these thoughts out of your mind. Body
sensations, thoughts and noises may distract
you. Part of learning to meditate is gaining the
ability to overcome these intrusions. If your
attention starts to wander see it as an object
you can guide and bring it back to your space.
Lay it gently at your feet and concentrate on
silencing your mind.

7

Meditation requires the strength of mind to
focus our thoughts. Eventually the process
becomes unceasing even when one is engaged
in work. In this way one works more
productively as one is distracted less.

8

An easy way to reduce stress fast

Breathe deeply. Take three slow, deep breaths using your diaphragm to breathe in through your nose, hold for about two seconds, then slowly exhale through your mouth. When we are under stress, we tense up, constricting the flow of oxygen into our body. Taking slow, deep breaths carries oxygen throughout our bodies and results in our feeling centred, having released stress. Providing your body with much-needed oxygen releases tension and stress fast.

9

To meditate, still your mind and empty it of all thought. When the mind is left without anything to cling to, it becomes still, and by making your mind still you will be calm.

10

You must be the change you wish to see in the world.

Mahatma Gandhi, early 20th century

11

Try to attain a relaxed state by developing the ability to separate yourself from your thoughts and problems. If you can learn to put these things outside yourself as objects, you can deal with them as separate entities and minimize their negative impact on you. This will enable you to approach life with a calmer, stronger state of mind.

12

Meditation is the process of sticking to one thought. That single thought keeps away other thoughts which would distract you. By constant meditation your ability to concentrate is strengthened and you become able to be completely focused whenever you need to be.

13

Sit quietly wherever you are and hold your mind on one thought. Be fully conscious, be aware of your surroundings and the people around you, but don't merge your consciousness with the environment. By taking this time out you will refresh your thinking for the task ahead.

14

Close your eyes and imagine you are walking in the countryside as it snows. Concentrate on hearing the quietness and feeling the stillness around you. Keep the feeling with you and spend five to ten minutes in this place. When you return to your surroundings you will be calmer and more focused.

15

There is meditation with thoughts, and there is meditation without thoughts. Successful meditation with the mind ultimately leads to meditation without the mind. Meditation helps you to control your mind's thinking.

Buddha, 560–480 BC

16

Try meditating on an event that is going to
happen, visualize it as you want it to turn out.
You have the power to mould it according to
your thought. Meditating on things bestows
power over them. In this way you can improve
your life.

17

When you have a problem, meditate on it and
the answer will come – during the meditation
or afterwards. If you meditate daily it will
soon become a habit and you will find yourself
a calmer person.

18

The meditating mind is free of all thoughts.
Concentrate your mind without distraction
and you will feel peaceful and refreshed.

19

A short centering exercise

❖ Bring your attention to the physical act of
breathing. Breathe naturally and bring
your attention to a part of your body.

❖ Pay attention to the changes there as a
result of breathing, for example the rising
and falling of the abdomen.

❖ Concentrate on this until you feel more
together and calmer. This can be done in
the car, at work or even out shopping and
is a useful quick meditation.

20

In order to hasten the awareness of the inner consciousness it is recommended that you become more aware of your thoughts as they arise and pass through your mind throughout the day. Don't get carried away with them, remain focused and uninvolved. Stay deeply aware of the consciousness that looks at these thoughts. Let peace fill you completely.

21

Someone with much experience of meditation can meditate anywhere and under all circumstances, but a beginner needs a quiet place to meditate. If you are a beginner, find a quiet area at home where you are relatively free from disturbance.

22

- ❖ Sit at ease in any posture.
- ❖ Close your eyes.
- ❖ Immediately after closing your eyes, watch whatever space you see inside.
- ❖ In the middle of this space, make an imaginary center of any size.
- ❖ Begin to repeat "I am blissful" as if the words are coming from that center to your eyes.
- ❖ Focus your attention on the last humming sound of each word spoken. If any thought or many thoughts arise, persist or subside during this period, remain neutral, just watching. Gently focus your attention.
- ❖ Continue meditating and holding this realization for five to ten minutes.

23

He who knows enough is enough will always have enough.

Lao Tse, 6th century BC

24

Imagine yourself standing on a beach, watching the waves crashing onto the shore. Feel the sea breeze and smell the salt water. Concentrate on the feeling of calmness that you experience now. Stay with this image and feeling for a while. This is a simple meditation to make you feel stronger, more centered and more in control.

25

If you have troublesome, worrying thoughts close your eyes and breathe deeply and slowly. Allow your worrying thoughts to come. With this meditation your thoughts are ignored or float by. You allow these thoughts and feelings to come in one side and out the other, like a banner being pulled by an aeroplane across the sky. Watch them leave you. Each time they come repeat the process until you feel ready to let them go completely.

26

After meditating, practise concentrating and stilling your mind for five minutes every day. The confusion of thoughts in the mind slow down not only during meditation but also in daily life. This will make you happier with a sharpened ability to concentrate. The ability to enjoy the present moment increases and you may also find that you are less critical of yourself and others.

27

The concentration involved in meditation is a way to develop the ability to pay attention to one object or subject while preventing the mind from running around. The practice itself strengthens the powers of concentration.

28

See your mind as being like a light bulb covered with many sheets. In meditation we need to peel away these sheets – whether they be thoughts, emotions, memories or sounds – to get to our inner light. Close your eyes and concentrate on getting to that glowing light bulb.

29

Rid yourself of delusions. Good thoughts keep bad thoughts away. When you think good thoughts they draw people towards you.

30

In contemplation recall the face of the poorest and the weakest man whom you have seen and ask yourself if the step you contemplate is going to be of any use to him. In this way may you become enlightened and enlightening.

Buddhist

31

Sit or lie down and relax your body, feelings and thoughts. Take some deep rhythmical breaths, breathing in through your nose and out through your mouth using your diaphragm until you feel relaxed. Now try to look at your thoughts as if they are not yours; see them rise in front of your eyes. Watch your thoughts calmly without being carried away by them or being emotionally involved with them. Do this for ten minutes each day or whenever you feel the need to take some time out.

32

Whenever you feel tired and stressed you must try to stop thinking and just be. Close your eyes and feel your being without thoughts and personality. Separate yourself from your stresses by placing them in your mind in a bag at your feet. You can deal with them calmly; they are not part of you.

33

One needs earnestness, persistence and strong motivation to succeed in meditation. The rewards are great and valuable. After the mind becomes habitually calm and quiet as a result of regular practice inner peace may be experienced throughout the day.

34

Quick visualization meditation

Imagine watching a candle flame. When a thought comes into your brain let it pass through. Don't argue or try to solve anything. If this occurs, focus again on the flame. Try saying a mantra.

A mantra is a word or sound to repeat over and over again to help you focus, for example, "Calm . . . calm . . .". Focus on your breathing – 1, 2, 3, 3, 2, 1. Repetition of slow breathing will help you to focus as well as pumping more oxygen into your body. Do this for up to 15 minutes each day.

35

Count to ten

If you are in a stressful situation and you feel it is getting really bad, count to ten slowly to give yourself time to think about the best way to react.

36

Tricks of meditation

Often, using a repetitive sound helps to focus the mind during meditation and to make unwanted thoughts float away. Some people simply focus on breathing, others think of a colour.

37

A calm mind which is not disturbed by hundreds of thoughts makes you more attentive to the issues at hand. Calm your thoughts, meditate daily, and soon your inner strength and mind power will grow.

38

Breathing and shaking

Standing, concentrate on shaking your body
from the inside out. Shake every part of your
body including fingers and toes. Try to
breathe deeply while doing this and
concentrate your mind to avoid unwanted
thoughts. Repeat this for five minutes every
day.

39

Be ye therefore merciful, as your Father also is
merciful.

Judge not, and ye shall not be judged:
condemn not, and ye shall not be condemned:
forgive, and ye shall be forgiven: give, and it
shall be given unto you; good measure, pressed
down, and shaken together, and running over,
shall men give into your bosom. For with the
same measure that ye mete withal it shall be
measured to you again.

Luke 6: 36–38

40

Take a breathing break. All you need to do is spend a minute or two doing a breathing exercise. It can be as simple as inhaling and exhaling deeply. This will always produce a calming effect.

41

I learned good morals and the government of my temper.
I learned endurance of labour, to want little and to work with my own hands.
I learned how to receive from friends what are esteemed favours, without being either humbled by them or letting them pass unnoticed.
I learned self-government, and cheerfulness in all circumstances.

Ancient Roman chant

42

All meditations begin with stillness and serenity.
Go to a quiet place. Begin by relaxing your body
and your mind. Take a few deep breaths, and
each time you exhale feel your body relax into a
peaceful state. Let go of your worries and cares.
Feel only the presence of calm within you.
Enjoy this feeling as you progress through the
meditation. If you find yourself becoming
anxious or thinking of other things, bring your
thoughts back to calmness. Let the words of the
meditation inspire you as you say them either
silently or aloud.

43

Write it down

Writing can be good therapy. If you're
overloaded with worries, take a pencil and
paper and spend 20 minutes writing down
your concerns and possible solutions to the
problems.

44

Sit upright on a chair or on the floor. Feel the sensation that your body is firmly planted on the earth, your hands resting easily, your heart soft, your eyes closed gently. Set free unwanted thoughts. Concentrate on the sensations of breathing. Take a few deep breaths to sense where you can feel the breath most easily. Let your breathing become natural. Relax into each breath as you feel it.

45

Humility is crucial to one's journey through life, but it is truly difficult to be humble. To try to see everyone through the eyes of others is one way to develop humility.

46

Concentrating

Start by learning to relax your body and clear your mind. Imagine all of your thoughts draining out of your body starting with the top of your head and working your way down to your feet. At this point let the thoughts flow out of you like water from a faucet.

47

With meditation, most people find the intrusion of random thoughts difficult to master at first. The point is not to try to make them stop – trying to stop random thoughts from entering your head and trying to make them go away is the very reason why they hang around and prevent you from concentrating. Think about the now – notice your troublesome random thoughts then release them and bring your mind back to the present. To meditate one must give the mind something else to do.

48

Meditation for guidance

❖ Visualize going through a series of curtains in the colours of the rainbow, the first one red, the second one orange and so on.

❖ As you go through the curtains close each one behind you.

❖ Behind the violet curtain are your spiritual guides. They will guide you in the direction you need to go.

❖ When you have finished meditating return to your curtain. Exit the curtains in the reverse order that you entered (violet, indigo, blue, green, yellow, orange, red) and remember always to close the curtains behind you.

49

Test for an open mind

Put your finger underneath your nose and exhale loudly. If more air is coming out of one nostril than the other then your mind is not fully open. Balance your breath by alternate nostril breathing.

50

Meditation can free and open our minds

With meditation we can expand the boundaries of our minds. The concentration involved in meditation benefits our performance in many areas helping us to move beyond the previous limitations of our personalities. Tense muscles become looser and we feel less constricted generally.

51

Change your behaviour through meditation

Because meditation is practised throughout changing conditions of the mind (thoughts, images, emotions) that we all experience every day, it is possible to channel these emotions and thoughts into different reaction patterns as our meditation techniques improve.

52

Meditation when anxious

Keep your focus in the present moment. Panicky thoughts usually express fears about an anticipated event, something that has yet to occur and in actuality may never happen. By directing your thoughts from an anticipated future event toward the present moment, you will help your mind stay calm and your body will follow suit.

53

Visualization exercise to calm your nerves

Familiarize yourself with these steps. When you're ready, spend the next ten to 15 minutes creating the scenery of your choice in your mind.

1. Sit or lie down in a comfortable position. Close your eyes.
2. Create an image in your mind of some place where you felt truly relaxed, calm, and happy.
3. In this picture, observe what is happening there. Notice the colours of the scenery. Notice the quiet atmosphere, or freshness of the air. Notice the shapes of familiar objects, and be aware of any movement that occurred.
4. Just let yourself recall the positive feelings in that scene. Enjoy what you remember and what you see in your mind's eye. Breathe deeply and relax.

54

Relaxation exercise

❖ Begin by taking slow, deep breaths. Repeat these messages to yourself.

❖ My hands and arms are heavy and warm (repeat five times).

❖ My feet and legs are heavy and warm (repeat five times).

❖ My abdomen is warm and comfortable (repeat five times).

❖ My breathing is deep and even (repeat ten times).

❖ My heartbeat is calm and regular (repeat five times).

❖ My forehead is cool (repeat five times).

❖ When I open my eyes, I will remain relaxed and refreshed (repeat three times).

55

Focus your mind

❖ Sit in an upright position (you may lie down if sitting is impossible). Try to align your spine so it is straight, relax your shoulders and place your hands in your lap. Close your eyes.

❖ Feel the sensations of your hands in your lap and your feet on the floor.

❖ Pay attention to all the sensations in your body then gradually let them go one by one.

❖ Pay attention to your breathing and concentrate on feeling it in your abdomen.

❖ Feel your thoughts as waves in the sea, allowing them to come and go.

❖ Be aware of feelings such as anger, fear, sadness or happiness.

❖ Continue to let these thoughts go.

❖ Open your heart to the present moment.

❖ Practise this for five to ten minutes each day.

56

Relaxing your body

- ❧ Rotate your head by rolling it on your shoulders to the left and right. Repeat five times in each direction, then reverse the directions for another five times.
- ❧ Move your hips to the left as you inhale and to the right as you exhale. Again, repeat five times then change direction to the right as you inhale and to the left as you exhale for another five times.
- ❧ Rotate your knees in a full circle with your feet touching each other, clockwise then anticlockwise for five times each.

57

Take a bath

Add some soothing music and scented bath oil and let your stress just melt away!

58

Physical meditation exercise to induce calm

Lie on the floor. Mentally bring your awareness to each part of your body and consciously relax it, progressively, from your feet all the way to the top of your head. Your breath should be full and relaxed. Use the following technique on each part of your body.

❖ Bring your awareness to your legs.
❖ Inhale deeply and lift one leg up, slightly tensing the foot and leg. Tense up more.
❖ Exhale and let the leg drop gently. Roll the leg from side to side and relax.
❖ Repeat the same for the other leg and foot and the rest of your body.

59

Walking meditation

If you are walking indoors, walk in a circle
anticlockwise, be aware of each breath as
you place each foot in front of the other. If
you are outside, do the same thing in a
straight line. Notice and let go of each thought
as they arise each time returning to focusing
on your footsteps. You can do this walk for
15–20 minutes.

60

Meditation must be undertaken with a non-
judgmental attitude and an open mind.

61

The purpose of life is being happy. Inner peace is the key. In that state of mind you can face difficulties with calm and reason, while keeping your inner happiness.

The Dalai Lama

62

Focus on your breathing: in . . . out . . . in . . . out. When you connect with each deep breath and place awareness on your body you will learn to focus on the moment and experience inner joy and peace in the present moment. You will develop skills for listening, managing stress and generating compassion.

63

You can meditate sitting or standing, even moving around. When focusing on each breath learn to notice your unfolding experience without judgement and with an open heart. Feel your physical sensations as they affect your body, then let the sensations flow away by concentrating on your breathing.

64

The three principles of meditation

1. Investigate and notice all events around you, including sounds and feelings.
2. Accept what you find.
3. Free yourself from these events by letting them go.

65

Reducing stress

❖ Create a quiet place for yourself and sit comfortably. Both feet should be touching the ground.

❖ As you relax your body will sink deeper into the chair and feel heavier.

❖ If your mind begins to wander, return to focusing on your breathing.

❖ You will become aware that your mind is clear. Don't allow any intrusive thoughts to affect your ability to relax. You begin to feel the quietness around you.

❖ Continue this as long as you are able to, anywhere between five and 30 minutes.

❖ As your meditation ends you will feel as if you are waking up.

❖ Sit very still for a moment and take several deep breaths.

❖ You are ready to begin your day.

66

The main steps to meditation

- ❖ Be aware of and sense your body.
- ❖ Connect deeply with your breathing and give yourself up to it.
- ❖ Pay attention to your thoughts and feelings.
- ❖ Open your heart to all that you discover.

67

Deep breathing

Practise deep breathing anywhere – while you're meditating, doing yoga, waiting to give a speech, or in your car stuck in traffic. Most forms of meditation include some type of breathing practice. Breathing deeply and slowly helps you calm down and feel more relaxed. There are several ways to practise deep breathing, but the idea is to do it slowly and mindfully.

68

For strength

❖ Sit in a chair with both feet firmly on the
   ground.
❖ Rest your arms by your sides and take
   some deep, even breaths.
❖ As your breathing becomes deeper,
   imagine yourself standing with your feet
   apart, hands by your sides with your
   fingers naturally open.
❖ With your breathing, relax your body and
   clear your mind.
❖ Imagine that there is a circle of energy or
   light by your spine.
❖ Through this light you are strong,
   connected to the Earth and you love and
   care for yourself.

69

Visualization to reduce stress

With this technique, also known as guided imagery, you are the director of your dream. Think of a peaceful, beautiful setting and imagine yourself there. Once you've pictured yourself in your safe and beautiful place, stay with your vision for several minutes, until you feel your mind and body relax. You can practise visualization at home or in your office, while out shopping or on the train. Guided imagery reduces stress by giving us greater control over our imaginations.

70

To help with creativity

❖ Make yourself comfortable in a chair with both feet on the ground.

❖ Take some deep, even breaths and with your breathing, relax your body and clear your mind.

❖ As you breathe, visualize a circle of light near your navel area. This is the energy source of your creativity and the beginning of your spirituality.

❖ As you concentrate feel your creative energy flow around you urging you to have faith in your ideas and your abilities.

71

Deepen your experience of meditation

As a "pre-meditation" preparation, bring your attention to the physical act of breathing. Breathe naturally, and with each cycle of breath bring your attention to a different part of your body, paying attention to the changes there as a result of the breathing. What do you do between breaths? Is there a pause? Consider each part of your body, one at a time, and move on.

72

For enlightenment

❖ Make yourself comfortable in a chair with both feet on the ground.

❖ Take some deep, even breaths and with your breathing, relax your body and clear your mind.

❖ As you breathe visualize a circle of light on the top of your head. This is the energy of enlightenment and true understanding of the world.

❖ As you concentrate on this light, events and emotions become clear and make sense. You find your true place in the world and know your true self.

73

The energy sources of the different parts of the body guide you to listen to their requests for attention through physical sensations:

Head – understanding and enlightenment
Forehead – imagination and self-awareness
Throat – guidance and wisdom
Heart – love and caring
Navel – creativity
Pelvic area – emotions and balance
Spine – strength

Trust that these sensations mean something – that positive energy flow is being blocked. You need to notice these connections in order to bring more vitality to all that you do.

74

Guide to restore balance in your life

❧ Sit comfortably and close your eyes,
keeping your feet on the floor.

❧ Allow scenes from your life to pass through
your mind and choose to concentrate on
one that appeals to you.

❧ Focus on this scene for several moments,
noticing colour, shape, texture and the
mood this image evokes in you.

❧ Become aware of the emotions you feel as
you look at this picture and let your mind
let go of all other thoughts.

❧ Allow yourself to relax and enjoy the
calmness of this moment. It is a feeling
you can return to whenever you need to
feel secure and at peace.

75

Pure consciousness is finding the place where there is no thought.

Buddhist

76

Transforming meditations

Meditation is a method for acquainting our minds with virtue. The more familiar our minds are with virtue, the calmer and more peaceful they become. When our minds our peaceful we are free from worries and mental discomfort and we experience true happiness. If we train our minds to become peaceful we will be happy all the time, even in the most adverse conditions. If our minds are not peaceful, even if we have the most pleasant external conditions we shall not be happy. Therefore it is important to train our minds through meditation.

77

Close your eyes and sit or lie down comfortably. Relax your body and mind and concentrate on letting your spirit soar high. Set it free to float in a blissful state of peace.

78

Walking meditation

❖ Set off walking alone, taking deep breaths and steady strides.

❖ As your breathing and walking pace become in tune with each other begin consciously to turn your mind off and concentrate on breathing.

❖ Concentrate on your breathing, inhaling for two or three steps then exhaling for the next two or three.

❖ Dismiss any unwanted thoughts and concentrate on matching your walking pace and your breathing.

79

Meditation for compassion

Begin by contemplating the various sufferings experienced by living beings until a strong feeling of compassion arises in your heart. When this feeling arises meditate on it in a single-minded way. If the feeling fades, or if your mind wanders on to another object, you should return to the first stage (contemplation) to bring the feeling back to mind. When the feeling has been restored, once again hold on to the feeling with single-minded concentration. This will help in all dealings with people, especially in the home and in the workplace.

80

Find your guide

❖ Allow your body to gently relax and get comfortable in your chair.

❖ Now move down into a safe place deep within yourself. From your safe, sacred space move into the corridor of your mind. Along the corridor are many doors and around one particular door is a golden light. Move through this door into a place of peace and comfort.

❖ Beyond this door you will find yourself in a beautiful, peaceful scene. You come to a body of water that is pure, clean and clear. You drink from this water and you are comforted and refreshed. You can hear gentle music and in the distance you see a golden light approaching you.

❖ This light will be your guide for whatever issue concerns you at this time. You should put your questions to the light.

❖ When you feel you have your answers, thank the light and retrace your steps back to the present as you sit in your chair.

81

Be aware of your self

❖ As you meditate be conscious of your
breathing and your posture.

❖ Notice the flow of energy through your
body.

❖ See your thoughts and their source.

❖ Know the value of action and reaction.

❖ Feel the rhythm of your body as it finds its
balance in the universe.

82

When you meditate, in order to put things
into perspective, always try to remember the
whole when dealing with a part. This way the
sense of calmness is increased as the unity of
all things is held in the mind.

83

Fulfil your potential

❖ Sit comfortably with both feet on the floor, close your eyes and concentrate on your breathing.

❖ Move your body so it is in a comfortable position with your spine straight, your palms facing up, and your feet flat on the floor.

❖ Continue to breathe deeply as you proceed with your meditation.

❖ Bring to mind an image of your own personal place of peace. In this place you can realize your full potential. Use all your senses to see what you are really like and what your best qualities are. See this potential unfolding in everything you've learned so far.

❖ You can come back anytime you want to enjoy the peace of this place and commune with your full potential self whenever you need to give your all to the task at hand.

84

The best time to meditate

In general it is best to meditate early in the morning directly after wakening and before starting your day. Early morning generally has fewer distractions than later in the day. Some people believe that it is good to meditate between 2 and 4 am but unless you are normally awake at that time, your normal waking time is preferable.

85

Close your eyes when you meditate

When you open your eyes you see the external world. When you close your eyes, you can divert your attention to your own inner self. Therefore in meditation you should always close your eyes.

86

Breathing

❖ Sit with your back straight and your feet on the floor.

❖ Try to pay attention to the breath going in and out of your nose.

❖ It does not matter if your breathing is deep or shallow, relaxed or not. Try simply to observe your breath.

❖ Notice when air enters your nose and when it leaves. If your mind wanders, bring it back to your breath. The goal is to accept your breathing, to breathe without caring how you breathe. As you practise and accept your breathing, it will improve.

87

Keep an open mind

An open mind is the key to wisdom and the
door to your innermost self during times of
meditation.

88

Focusing

❖ In order to focus more easily, some people
count their breaths up to four.
❖ The first time they exhale, they count one.
The next time they exhale, they count two.
❖ After they count the fourth exhalation,
they go back to one.
❖ If this method works for you, good, but if
you find you are concentrating on
counting rather than breathing you are
probably better off not using this method.

89

Bringing the benefits of meditation into your life

Acceptance is key. Think about an unpleasant situation – being stuck in a traffic jam for example. You may feel upset about the delay and angry with yourself for not checking the traffic reports. See things that you can't control, like the traffic, and try to accept them as they are. Observe how the anger or frustration affects you physically while you are experiencing it and learn to accept and prevent these physical sensations.

90

Use negative experiences to develop your attitude of acceptance. As you begin to realize that these negative experiences can be useful, it starts to feel like there is a positive side to everything so you don't see things as so bad in all of your life's stresses.

91

On receptivity

Most meditations involve a sense of receptivity to an external source. One can imagine that one is receiving energy from an outside source, in the form of light for example, which can then flow through us and even radiate from us as it flows on towards others.

92

Dealing with episodes of depression

If you feel one of the mental states characterized by depression – worthlessness, helplessness, unhappiness or anxiety – then you need to start by looking for a sense of contentment to begin from where you are now. You need to learn to work from within your mental state.

A common technique is simply to repeat, "I want to be well, I want to be happy, I want to be free from suffering". You can do this while openly experiencing anxiety. The important thing is to acknowledge the emotion and not to try to manufacture an emotion to replace it.

93

Visualizing protection

A useful way of dealing with anxiety and with
a sense of being overwhelmed by the outside
world is to visualize a protective sphere around
you. This protective sphere surrounds you as a
safe space. Your subconscious will react to
your having a safe space around you as if it is
really there and you can find that this becomes
a useful technique when facing difficult
situations.

94

Meditation is based on the recognition and
acceptance that change is a universal truth.
Meditation helps us to recognize that we
always have the power to influence and change
our experience.

95

Posture

Sit in an easy posture for an hour in the
morning in a natural way. Your posture
should always be the same and you should
make sure you are perfectly comfortable. The
upright position, keeping a straight but not
rigid spine, is generally thought to be the best.
It can be in a chair or on the floor.

96

As a preparation for meditation, bring your
attention to the physical act of breathing.
During meditation you are aiming for simple
awareness, nothing else. Meditation is a time
to connect to your inner self and let go of the
issues and roles we get caught up in, such as
work and parenting concerns and
responsibilities. It may be that your meditation
on any particular day is peaceful, or it may be
fretful and full of worried thoughts.
Regardless, if you meditate daily it will have a
positive effect on your life.

97

Devise your own personal mantra

A mantra is a sound, word, or phrase that is repeated to yourself in meditation. It could be spoken aloud, as a chant, or silently, as in meditation. A mantra is used as a way of displacing everyday thoughts and shifting awareness inwards.

The correct process of meditation involves the rhythmic, silent chanting of a mantra, either a universal one or a personal one. A personal mantra is one that you have devised, either by yourself or with the help of your spiritual teacher, through dealing with your own issues of acceptance and progress.

Through the use of your mantra and positive visualization, your mind will gradually identify with the blissful self within.

98

Meditation using a mantra

Sit comfortably in a quiet place with your feet firmly on the floor. Close your eyes and breathe naturally. Sit for about one minute before you begin thinking the mantra to allow your heart and breathing to become calm and even.

Breathe through your nose, allowing the breath to flow in rhythm with your lungs. Feel peaceful and at rest. Consciously relax your whole body. Gently bring your attention to your breath and begin to think the mantra, gently and easily. Just let it come and allow yourself to be absorbed in it – don't force it. Allow your thoughts and feelings to come and go. Don't try to control them in any way – just notice them.

99

Accept all things in your life, both good and bad

You cannot change the present. If you learn to accept this, you are on the path to freeing yourself from the useless energy involved in resistance. Meditation can help your mind to become more flexible, making you stronger in the face of adversity.

100

Avoid being self-righteous and feeling that you are wise enough. Accept that you have much to learn and that there are many to teach you.

101

Integrity

Be sure of your own mind and the integrity of your decisions.

Do not do to others things you do not want done to you.

In loving, you will be loved.

In hating, you will be hated.

In giving, you will receive.

In accepting, you will be accepted.

102

Feelings

Our feelings are born out of our needs.

When we are afraid, we need to be safe and secure.

When we love, we have a need to be loved.

When we hate, we need to have things our way and only our way.

When we are sad, we need to fill an empty space within.

The happy person is content with who he is and what he has.

103

Meditation for pain

Practise breathing until you are in a state of calm. Imagine you are lying in the sun, on a beach, for example, or in a field or garden. As you feel the light bathing you in its warmth, start to reconnect your mind with the physical sensations of your body. Concentrate on the area of your body that is painful and focus the warm sunlight on that area. Feel the warmth relax you and soothe you. Enjoy the sense of calm and peace.

104

Be forgiving

Don't ask for forgiveness only when it is expected of you, or be forgiving only when it is expected of you. Ask for forgiveness when you realize your actions require it. You should offer forgiveness of the actions of others when it is requested sincerely.

105

Burmese position for meditation

In the Burmese position for meditation the legs are crossed and both feet rest flat on the floor. The knees should also rest on the floor, though sometimes it takes a bit of practice to be able to get the legs to drop that far. After a while the muscles will loosen up and the knees will begin to drop. To help that happen push your body forwards a little bit. By imagining the top of your head pushing upward to the ceiling and by stretching your body that way, you can get your spine straight and then let the muscles go soft and relax. With your stomach pushing out a little, there will be a slight curve in the lower region of the back. In this position, it takes very little effort to keep the body upright and comfortable. This is a Zazen meditation, in other words sitting cross-legged.

106

A quick way of dealing with intrusive thoughts during meditation

If other thoughts start to intrude, picture them as being written on a clear board between you and your focal thought, then picture them being erased from that board as they might be from a piece of paper. Deal with any thought, other than your focal thought, quickly. Try to maintain concentration on your focal thought for at least five minutes. Picture and experience it as if it were real. By doing this you can create a more alert state for yourself at any time of day or in any circumstance.

107

Controlling your breathing

Start by taking a deep breath in through your
nose and hold it for the count of four. Then
let it all out slowly through your mouth.
Repeat this until you begin to feel relaxed. Let
your breathing settle into a steady, rhythmic
state. This simple technique alone can relax
and refresh you at any time. If you are only
doing the breathing exercise, it is not necessary
to go through any visualization process.

108

Fate

In meditation all things return to their source,
the single form of energy from which they
were created.

109

A simple breathing meditation

Sit comfortably in a chair. The most
important thing is to keep your back straight
to prevent your mind from becoming sluggish
or sleepy. Become aware of the sensation of
your breath as it enters and leaves the nostrils.
This sensation is the object of meditation.
Remain focused single-mindedly on the
sensation of your breath.

Gradually your distracting thoughts will
subside and you will experience a sense of
inner peace and relaxation. Your mind will feel
lucid and spacious and you will feel refreshed.

110

When meditating on some anxiety or issue,
you should find that the source of your
problems also provides the solution to them.

111

Getting into a comfortable position

If you are lying down, be sure your back and neck are properly supported so as not to tire your body. If you are sitting, be sure that both feet are flat on the floor and that you are sitting as erect as possible without being too stiff or strained. Relax your shoulders and abdomen. You should have your arms resting comfortably in your lap with palms up.

112

Your surroundings

Your surroundings are directly related to how you feel. If you are content to have them decay then you are happy for yourself to decay. If you protect and care for your surroundings, you are protecting and caring for yourself.

113

To rejuvenate you and attune you with the energies of the Earth

Stand straight with your hands at your sides and place your feet together. Close your eyes and imagine a bright, white energy source shaped like a ball situated in the centre of your head. Take a deep breath while continuing to see the white light ball. Exhale forcibly, moving the ball of light quickly through the inside of your body and down into the Earth. Imagine the energy light continuing to travel deep into the center of the Earth.

Then gradually begin to inhale – proceed slowly enough to feel the energy rising up from the Earth, through your body and back into the centre of your head.

Repeat this exercise at least three times.

114

How to integrate meditation into your daily life

Meditation should permeate your whole life. You should not allow a gulf to develop between your meditation and your daily life. The success of meditation depends upon the purity of your conduct outside the meditation session. Keep a watch over your mind at all times by applying mindfulness, alertness, and conscientiousness. Try to abandon whatever bad habits you may have. Deep experience of meditation is the result of practical training over a long period of time, both in and out of meditation. Therefore you should practise steadily and gently, without being in a hurry to see results.

115

Balance

When seeking balance in your life accept things you have done and accept what others may have done to you.

116

To focus your mind

First of all, seat yourself comfortably. A quiet place is preferable, but not essential. Close your eyes and breathe naturally. Sit for about one minute before you begin thinking the mantra to allow your heart and breathing to slow.

Repeat the mantra, "I am calm, I am focused, I am here."

Allow your thoughts and feelings to come and go with detachment. You may experience a deep state of relaxation but don't worry if you don't.

When you have finished, take about a minute to slowly return to normal awareness. Be gentle with yourself when opening your eyes or ending meditation.

117

You must exercise your mind, body and spirit. For them all to function at their best you must neglect none of them.

118

When you meditate, visualize what you want to the point of it becoming a reality. For example, before an important job interview visualize yourself as successful and prosperous. The technique of creative visualization deals with the premise that we all create our own reality and therefore have the power to change many aspects of that reality.

119

If you want true happiness, you have to find it in the present. You have your body, sitting here and breathing. You have your mind, thinking and aware. Bring these things together. Think about your breath and be aware of it as it comes in and goes out. Keeping your thoughts directed to your breath is mindfulness. Being aware of the breath as it comes in and out is alertness. Keep those two aspects of the mind together to strengthen your concentration and alertness and thereby enjoy living in the moment, bringing you happiness.

120

Learn humility

Never be dismissive of another person, alive or
dead. Never hold yourself in high esteem in
relation to others. Don't judge others as
lacking beside you in any situation.

Buddha, 560–480 BC

121

For wisdom

❖ Make yourself comfortable in a chair with
both feet on the ground.
❖ Take some deep, even breaths and with your
breathing, relax your body and clear your
mind.
❖ As you breathe, visualize a circle of light at
your throat. This energy is your voice of
guidance and wisdom.
❖ Concentrate on listening to this energy to
lead you to take actions that are balanced
and true to yourself.

122

Trust your instincts

❖ Sit in a quiet place and make sure you are comfortable.

❖ Place both feet on the ground. Close your eyes. Concentrate on your breathing.

❖ Imagine yourself in a walkway that is narrow with clean blank walls on either side.

❖ Walk along until you come to an opening in the wall. Go through this opening and see you are in a safe, quiet space that is yours and yours alone.

❖ When you are ready you will become aware of another presence in your space. Ask any questions you have and wait for the answer – it will come.

❖ This is your inner messenger and you can return to it at any time you like. It is your intuition and part of your life.

123

Be aware that positive company will be a positive influence on you and that negative company will be a negative influence on you. Being with kind people will make you kind and being among hateful people will bring out hatefulness in you.

124

Do not think in terms of there being a nothing. Once you can recognize something as nothing it has already become something.

Buddhist

125

To feel peace and serenity

Pick a quiet place and sit quietly with both
feet on the ground. Relax and concentrate on
your breathing. Think of a place you find very
beautiful and while picturing your beautiful
scene, be aware of your breathing. Start to
walk into the place you have pictured until
you come upon a place where you'd like to sit
down for a while. See yourself sitting in this
beautiful place. See yourself as part of this
beauty and feel the peace. With each breath,
relax deeper into this scene and stay for as long
as you like. When you know it is time to
leave, rise and begin to walk back.

126

The half-lotus position

In the half-lotus, the left foot is placed on the right thigh and the right leg is tucked underneath. This position is slightly asymmetrical and sometimes the upper body needs to compensate in order to keep itself absolutely straight. This is a good way to loosen and stretch the leg muscles. This is another cross-legged Zazen meditation.

127

To meditate is to focus your mind on one thought, idea, or concept. It may also mean, to revolve an idea in your mind so as to change the way in which you think of that idea. Meditation is, therefore, a tool with which you may manipulate thought in an organized manner.

128

Test for relaxation

Stand up. Bring one hand directly in front of your body. Let your wrist go limp and move your hand up and down, following the line of your spine. Close your eyes and consciously relax. Allow your head to be moved by the magnetic influence of your hand. The more consciously relaxed you are, the more powerful becomes the hand's magnetic influence.

Feel as if you are a puppet. As your hand moves up, your head follows the hand up, as if there is a string from your hand to your head. Occasionally, let your hand fall down. See that your whole body slumps slightly forward. When you pick your hand back up over your head, your whole body straightens up.

This exercise reflects how balanced your mind is, and how open to meditation you are. If there is any tension in your mind, your hand cannot fall swiftly, and neither can you relax.

129

Meditate for a better personal life

Meditation has a significant impact on your personal life:

❖ It gives you control over your "control room". By being able to control your thought processes you are able to banish negative thoughts and become happier.

❖ It develops detachment from the day-to-day world of forms and issues because in the meditative state they are outside you rather than inside.

130

Keep your home orderly, tidy and efficient as a reflection of your mind.

131

Talk to yourself

As you slowly breathe in, say to yourself, I am. As you breathe out, say slowly to yourself, calm.

Repeat this until your mind is calm and you can focus on your breathing.

132

To balance emotions

Make yourself comfortable in a chair with both feet on the ground. Take some deep, even breaths and with your breathing, relax your body and clear your mind.

Imagine that there is a circle of light by your pelvic area. This is your energy source of emotions and pleasure and contributes to overall balance in life.

Acceptance of this energy will bring feelings of joy in the present and stability to the emotions.

133

How to use a mantra

You should repeat the mantra in the mind at intervals of two to four seconds, though a longer interval may be suitable. The repetition should not accompany the breathing rhythm or heartbeat. From time to time the repetition may spontaneously start to follow these rhythms, but it is important not to try to attach the meditation sound to any rhythmical sensations in the body. During meditation the repetitive sound will partly shield you against external stimuli and induce an increased corresponding sensitivity towards internal processes making the meditation experience more profound.

134

Infinity can be contained within the finite.

Buddha, 560–480 BC

135

The rhythm of meditation

Without rhythm there would be no meditation. According to Buddhist teachings the soul controls its instrument (the body) by imposing a rhythm on it. First the rhythm, then gradually the mind and consciousness become attuned to your body's rhythm, usually through breathing. As this happens you should find that solutions to your problems come more easily to you.

136

Cleanse yourself

Imagine a transparent globe hovering about two feet above your head. Next, visualize a bright beam of light energy coming down from the globe and entering your head through the crown.

See and feel the light as it travels into your head, down your neck, and then through your shoulders. Picture it flowing through your veins and, as it does, feel it cleanse you and take away all your tiredness.

As it flows down further through the torso of your body feel it cleansing you. Picture it travelling lower down through your legs and out of your toes. You have become a light being. You feel lighter and can feel yourself gradually floating upwards towards the globe. As your head enters the globe you start to feel peace within yourself. You go up further until you are entirely within the globe, totally protected from any danger. You are totally relaxed and peaceful. Stay like this for about 15 minutes. Allow yourself to come back to consciousness slowly.

137

Take a break

Get a change of scenery by doing something simple. A walk outdoors can give you a new outlook on a situation. Look around you and notice colours, textures and sounds. Breathe deeply and be in the present.

138

Get back to nature

Nature can be a great stress-reducer. Drive to the countryside or seaside and take a walk. Stroll through a flower garden or nature trail. Listen to a tape of ocean sounds or birds. Relaxing for 15 minutes or more a day using these or any other techniques can go a long way towards relieving stress.

139

Breathing

To breathe successfully, keep your shoulders down and your chest forwards, and raise the corners of your mouth. Breathe slowly with deep abdominal breaths. As you inhale pull your stomach in and as you exhale push your stomach out. Breathe using the full capacity of your lungs and find a rhythm that is comfortable and relaxing for you. You should practise this for five to ten minutes each day.

140

Meditation can be used simply as a means to relax the body and mind. Our lives are full of tension and we tend to rush around never being still or gathering our thoughts. Learn to experience life in the moment at least once a day so you enjoy being in your life.

141

Chakras explained

Around your body there are chakras, or psychic centers. These are seen as different colours. Usually in the West we use seven chakras, although some in the East say there are nine. These all run up the front of your body, centrally, but they can also be seen from behind. The colors of the chakras are as follows:

- ❖ The crown (the top of the head) is purple
- ❖ The ejna or third eye (just above eyebrows in centre of forehead) is midnight blue
- ❖ The throat is sky blue
- ❖ The heart is green
- ❖ The solar plexus is yellow
- ❖ The spleen (just below the ribcage) is orange
- ❖ The base (groin) is red

142

Rhythmic breathing exercise to sharpen awareness

Sit comfortably, then begin rocking the body back and forth, slowly, in decreasing arcs, until you settle at your center of gravity. Begin by counting your breaths, counting each inhalation and each exhalation, beginning with one and counting up to ten. When you get to ten, come back to one and start again.

When you've been practising this breathing for a while, your awareness will sharpen. Next it's time to begin counting every cycle of the breath. Inhalation and exhalation will count as one, the next inhalation and exhalation as two.

Try to practise this every day for at least ten minutes.

143

Keep the following with you at all times:

* Peace
* Trust
* Friendships
* Inspiration
* Community
* Goodness
* Spiritual growth
* The sacred
* Celebration

144

Meditation in a chair

Often the most comfortable way to meditate is to sit in a chair with your feet flat on the floor. You can use a cushion in the same way you would use it on the floor, sitting on the forward third of it. It's very important to keep the spine straight with the lower part of the back curved. All of the aspects of the posture that are important when seated on the floor are just as important when sitting in a chair.

145

Meditation for answers to problems

Sit quietly, close your eyes and feel yourself surrounded by light. Hold in your mind the question that is troubling you. Visualize the words and concentrate your mind. The answer will come to you as a pure thought. Repeating this over a period of time will result in you becoming more decisive as your mind learns to visualize the answers.

146

Seiza position

In the seiza position you sit without a pillow, kneeling with the buttocks resting on the upturned feet which form an anatomical cushion. You can use a pillow to keep the weight off your ankles if you prefer. You can also use a seiza bench. It keeps all the weight off your feet and helps to keep your spine straight. This is another cross-legged Zazen meditation.

147

Meditating comfortably

Sit in a position that does not demand a significant amount of attention or strain. Sit comfortably on a chair, a sofa or a bed with firm support for the lower back. Keep surrounding stimuli (noise, light, etc.) to a minimum and close your eyes. It is best to meditate early in the morning if possible. Whatever kind of meditation you are doing, you need to repeat the meditation in your thoughts without strain and without concentration to focus your mind.

148

Meditation for strength

Begin by focusing on your breathing. As you slow your breathing, relax your entire body, from top to bottom.

Imagine that there is a white pitcher above your head. This pitcher is filled with bright, white light. The pitcher tilts and you are covered and filled completely with bright, white light.

Continue absorbing more light until you have a bubble of light spanning three feet around your body. You can stretch your arms out to each side and you are still surrounded by this bright, white light.

This light bubble is strong, protective, healthy, wise and vibrant with life. It is yours; it is you. From today, during moments when you feel timid, or vulnerable, or ill, remember your bright, white light.

149

Breathing meditation

Sit comfortably with your back straight.
Breathe in deeply and out deeply a few times
and focus on any area of your body where
your breathing is easy to notice and your mind
feels rested.

This could be your nose, your chest, your
abdomen, or any area at all. Stay with that
spot, noticing how it feels as you breathe in
and out. Don't force the breath – let it flow
naturally and notice how it feels. When you
feel that your breathing in your chosen area is
comfortable, shift your attention to another
part of your body and notice how your
breathing feels there. If you sense tension, try
to relax. If your breathing feels jagged or
uneven, try to breathe smoothly.

Continue this practice all over your body
until you feel truly relaxed.

150

Meditation for your own happiness

Sit comfortably upright in a balanced position.
Try not to lean forward or back, to the left or
the right. Close your eyes and say to yourself,
"May I be truly happy and free from
suffering."

It is important to realize that this is not
selfish and that there are good reasons for it. If
you can't wish for your own happiness you
can't honestly wish for the happiness of others.

Some people need to remind themselves
constantly that they deserve happiness and
believe it. If you don't believe it you will
constantly find ways to punish yourself and
end up punishing others in some way as well.

151

Meditation sound

Many people use a sound to aid meditation. This can be a hum, a chant or a particular sound that you find helpful when concentrating your mind. The sound should be repeated in your mind without effort. This is a useful method for achieving a greater degree of relaxation.

152

Focus your mind

One of the great benefits of meditation is to be able to focus your mind on what you choose to focus on, rather than being led by your mind. There is no time in your life when your brain is not engaged; the ability to focus your mind in this way is of enormous benefit in your daily life.

153

Become happier by strengthening your alertness

Begin to breathe in a way that's comfortable. Experiment to see what kind of breathing feels best for your body right now. It might be deep breathing, shallow breathing, long or short, heavy or light, fast or slow. Once you find a rhythm that feels comfortable, stay with it for a while.

Learn to savour the sensation of your breathing. Generally speaking, the smoother the texture of the breath, the better. Think of your breath as energy that flows through your body with each inhalation and exhalation. Learn to listen and respond to what your body is telling you right now. How can you best provide for that need? If you feel tired, try to breathe in a way that energizes the body. If you feel tense, try to breathe in a way that's relaxing. Do this for ten to 20 minutes each day.

154

A quick calming meditation

Sit yourself in a comfortable position which is easy to maintain, but don't lie down. Close your eyes. Keep note of each twitch or itch. Where in the body does it occur? Is it trying to tell you something? Feel yourself connected to the Earth through your hands and feet and concentrate on feeling nothing but a blissful state of peace.

155

Throughout your life your thoughts, feelings and beliefs change, sometimes radically, but you still exist as yourself. Ask yourself "Who am I?" Think about it, and then just try to be aware of the answer with no words or thoughts. The non-verbal answer is the point at which you reach the state of pure consciousness.

156

Close your eyes and see nothing but a blank white space in front of you. Do nothing but concentrate on your breathing. Even though you do not do anything, you are actually doing something. You are expressing yourself. You are expressing your true nature. Your eyes will express; your voice will express; your demeanor will express. The most important thing is to express your true nature in the simplest, most adequate way and to appreciate it in its smallest existence.

157

Never do to others what you would not like
them to do to you.

Confucius, 551–479 BC

158

May I be filled with loving kindness.
May I be well;
May I be peaceful and at ease.
May I be happy.

Ancient Tibetan Buddhist meditation

159

Sit quietly and look inside yourself to examine and be conscious of the feeling you have of yourself. Simply remain conscious of the feeling that you are alive, that you exist. Concentrate on what you feel is your essence, who you are. This knowledge is actually always with you, no matter what you are doing, or where you are but it often becomes clouded by sensations and by thoughts.

160

❖ For five minutes, lie on the floor and relax your body, breathing deeply. Concentrate on relaxing from your toes to the top of your head.

❖ Visualize yourself lying at the bottom of the ocean. There is nothing around you except sand.

❖ Each time you have a worry, see it as an air bubble and watch it float away from you.

❖ Repeat this until you feel calm and relaxed and ready to continue with your day.

161

When meditating, instead of thinking of ourselves as separated into multitudes of units, we need to see ourselves as a single whole being. This makes it much easier to concentrate.

162

See the beginning of the world as existence
that multiplied itself into innumerable forms
for the sheer delight of being. In this way feel
yourself connected to all things and you will
feel strong.

163

Making a meditation area

Dedicate an area of your home to meditation.
It doesn't have to be large, even a mantelpiece
or a shelf will do. It is preferable to have water
in it somehow – a bowl of water or even just a
picture of water will do. Include things which
are of personal value to you. This should be a
place where you feel at peace. Take off your
shoes when you visit your area and light a
candle as a mark of respect.

164

Problem-solving meditation

This problem-solving meditation takes the form of a ten-minute walk. Choose a familiar pathway and swing your arms at your sides in opposition to your legs. Mentally count the in-breath as 1, 2 and the out-breath as 3, 4. When your pattern of breathing is established, stop counting.

As your body warms up, your breathing will settle into its regular pattern and your thoughts will begin to clear. Imagine that ahead of you the sun is rising over the horizon. Walk along toward the sunrise feeling a rise in your energy and the growing warmth of sun. Let the sunlight clear any unpleasant thoughts and replace them with a question. "How can I deal with this issue?"

Take note of any answer that comes to mind which might solve your problem. Finally, take a deep breath. You should feel re-energized.

165

Insomnia

Meditation can be an effective weapon in fighting insomnia.

Lying in bed, focus on your breathing. Breathe in deeply and evenly and exhale slowly through your nose and mouth. In your mind, imagine yourself in a safe, secure place where no one can see you or knows you are there. In this place, imagine that your thoughts which keep you from sleep can't reach you either. See your thoughts trying to penetrate your space and failing, then melting away.

All the time notice your breathing. You are safe, you are protected, you can relax and go to sleep.

166

A quick way to meditate

Choose a quiet place. Sit upright and comfortably, keeping your back as straight as possible. Let each breath bring calmness and relaxation. Be aware of what feels closed up and tense in your mind, body and soul. Each time you breathe open up those closed feelings. Open your mind, your emotions and your senses. Notice whatever feelings, images and emotions come to you. Appreciate moments of stability and peace. Reflect on how emotions, feelings and stories appear and disappear. Focus on your body and rest for a moment. Meditate in this way for ten minutes.

167

Why meditate?

Meditation quietens the mind. If you are stressed at work or at home try this simple meditation.

Concentrate on your breathing – *in* and *out*, *in* and *out*. As your breathing deepens, your brainwaves slow. With this action your mind moves from being very active and unfocused to being calmer, more focused, and clearer-thinking. Blood flow to the brain increases, and concentration and memory improve. Meditating in this way should create a mood of calm.

168

Mindfulness meditation

Mindfulness meditation means becoming aware of the many things that we do automatically.

Begin with an awareness of your breath as it enters your nose. Focus on the sensation of your abdomen expanding as you breathe in. Shift your awareness to the air as you breathe out. This is focusing on the cyclical nature of breathing and should be practised for approximately 20 minutes a day, although you could begin with just five minutes a day.

169

Meditation as focus

In essence, meditation is focus. It involves directing your attention to one specific thing so that your state of mind changes. There are many things you can focus on and many ways to meditate. Among things to try are:

❖ Focus on what you are thinking or feeling in the current moment.

❖ Focus on a word (a mantra), a thought, something visual (a candle flame, an image, a symbol), a sound or your own breath.

❖ Focus on your body's controlled movement and breathing.

❖ Focus in turn on each of the body's 15 major muscle groups, tensing and then relaxing each in sequence.

There is no *wrong* way to meditate. Your experiences with meditation will vary from day to day so simply accept whatever occurs.

170

Quick meditation at your desk

✤ Sit upright and at ease in a comfortable chair. Close your eyes.

✤ With relaxed effort, focus your attention on your breathing.

✤ You might want to imagine that each inhalation is bringing health and vitality to your body, and each exhalation is releasing pain, stress, or illness.

✤ If your attention drifts away, bring it back gently and continue to observe your breathing.

✤ Continue this for five to ten minutes to feel refreshed and re-energized.

171

To energize you

Remove your socks and shoes. Position yourself for this exercise by standing with your feet about a yard apart and by holding your arms straight out to your sides.

Let your right palm face downwards and your left palm face upwards. Start breathing deeply and strongly. Be sure to inhale and exhale deeply and intensely. Visualize an energy of light moving into your solar plexus and building up there while also moving throughout your whole body. Simultaneously, picture the energy flowing into your left hand, through your center, and finally out of your right hand. Continue this visualization for a while.

You will know you have achieved the desired result of this meditation when you experience an energy rush often accompanied by a feeling of extreme peace.

172

Practise the breathing technique (slowly and evenly in and out) regularly and it will have a beneficial impact on your sense of well-being. Breathing is a bridge between the subconscious and conscious minds. This is because breathing is both subconscious (your body keeps breathing automatically whether you think about it or not), and conscious (you can take it out of "automatic" mode and consciously control it by breathing fast, slow and so on.

173

The chocolate meditation

Concentrate on a piece of chocolate fully as it slowly dissolves in your mouth. This can take up to five minutes. Think about the taste and the texture as it slowly melts. Eating such a tiny amount with full concentration actually means that you eat less of it so you can enjoy it without guilt or weight gain.

174

You can do this exercise either sitting up or lying down, just make sure your spine is straight. This meditation is to circulate energy around the centre of your torso, in synchronized co-ordination with your breathing.

Start by imagining an orange-sized width of glowing white light energy at the base of your spine. Then begin slowly to breathe in, while at the same time seeing the energy slowly moving up your spine. As you continue to breathe in, see it continuing up the spine, over the top of your head and down the center of your face to the upper lip. At that point, you begin slowly exhaling, and you see the energy go down from the lower lip, down the front of the chest to the groin, then back to the base of the spine.

At this point, continue the entire movement again without pausing. See the light as a complete circulation of energy that is moving all the time.

175

Meditation to bring love into your life

Begin by recalling the feeling of unselfish love.
The object of your affection could be a child,
an adult or even a household pet. Once you
have that feeling, try to hold on to it. Think of
someone you like but don't really love in the
same way. Think of them while at the same
time holding on to the feeling of
unconditional love.

Think of someone you don't like. Try to
feel unselfish love for their spirit (not their
personality or physical presence – especially if
they have been someone who has hurt you).
Widen your feeling of unconditional love to
embrace the whole of your world and hold
this feeling in your mind.

176

Breath counting

Seat yourself comfortably, keeping your spine as straight as possible. As you breathe start counting your inhalations and exhalations: one . . . two . . . one . . . two. The next time you inhale do the same thing, but this time count: two . . . two . . . two . . . two. Carry on counting silently until you get to ten, then start over again from one.

Breath counting will take time and patient practice to master, but it is an exercise that clears your mind for more conscious meditation. It can also help you to return to your work feeling more focused.

177

Think about your place in the world in relation to others. Nothing happens in isolation. All parts promote the whole.

178

To meditate while walking you should aim to synchronize your steps with your breathing. Set your pace and stride to whatever feels like a smooth, comfortable rhythm for you. For example, you might decide to inhale during the first two steps, hold your breath for the third, and exhale during the fourth and fifth, then repeat. Or you could inhale for five strides and exhale for five strides. The pattern is entirely up to you. If meditating while walking try to walk for at least five minutes and walk outside if at all possible.

179

A mirror exercise for concentration and self-discipline

This mirror exercise requires some equipment. It is best to practise this meditation in a darkened room lit only by one or two candles placed in front of your mirror. You should arrange the mirror so that you can see your entire face. Also, place the mirror one or two feet from your face.

You can sit either in a chair or on the floor as long as you keep your spine straight. Start the meditation by staring into the reflection in the mirror of your right eye. Try to avoid blinking. Perform this exercise for no less than ten minutes at a time.

180

Meditation for good will

Sit comfortably erect, without leaning forward
or backward, left or right. Close your eyes and
think thoughts of good will. Now spread good
will to other people. Begin with those who are
close to your heart, your family, your parents
and your very close friends: "May they find
true happiness". Then spread this good will
out in widening circles to include people you
know well, those you don't know so well,
people you like and even people you don't
like. Try to prevent any limitations on your
good will, thus preventing limitations on your
mind. Now spread thoughts of good will to all
living beings. "May they find true happiness
too".

181

Meditation for improving awareness and consciousness

Begin by inhaling deeply and exhaling deeply. Next, begin to inhale so slightly and gradually that you are barely aware you are inhaling at all. When you begin to feel the urge to actually take a breath, do so. Take one breath, then another, making sure you are exhaling deeply and fully as if releasing a big sigh. It is best to repeat this exercise for as long as possible.

This is a great meditation to do throughout the day to help return your consciousness back to true reality and improve your concentration.

182

Meditation for being kind

Every morning choose one person you know
to be your special daily focus. Try to choose
someone you are in regular contact with, such
as a spouse, child, friend, or co-worker. Make
a commitment to yourself to be very kind,
humble and thoughtful of this person for the
entire day. Take time during your day to think
about this person's life. Think about their
challenges, fears, and joys. Be attentive to
them. Next morning start all over with a new
person in your thoughts.

183

Sit with your spine straight or lie down. Relax and watch your body breathe. Keep your mind focused on the breath going in and out.

The trick is to let your subconscious mind control your breathing (as it does normally), but pay attention to your breathing.

This mediation requires a *passive* concentration. The result will be an improved ability to concentrate and increased calmness under pressure.

184

Meditation for chronic pain

Sit in the upright meditation position keeping your spine straight but not rigid. Concentrate on seeing a bright, warming light at the point of pain in your body. Feel this light warming the painful area. Many people find that regular use of this technique can reduce chronic pain.

185

Visualization

Visualizing allows the mind to wind down and expands awareness, which is one of the goals of meditation. Visualization is done with the *mind's eye*. When you are visualizing you are sensing with your entire consciousness, not merely one physical sense. Visualization is a form of knowledge of the object you are visualizing; it is focusing your awareness by using your entire consciousness. You will develop your understanding of what this means after practising the technique for some time.

186

Worrying and meditation

In some ways worrying and meditation are similar. To worry is to concentrate intently on something – in the same way that one does when meditating – but the object of attention in the case of worrying is something upsetting. In meditating, though, one tries not to "think". If we can succeed in this way to clear our minds of clutter, relevant and useful thoughts are able to emerge – thoughts that may have been there all along, but our minds have simply been too busy to be aware of them.

187

When your mind is at peace you will experience a form of calm, joyous consciousness different from everyday consciousness. This consciousness is a vast, endless space of calmness, happiness, joy and power.

188

Meditation to bring happiness to others

To spread good will to other living beings tell
yourself: "All living beings, no matter who
they are, no matter what they have done to me
in the past, may they all find true happiness
too".

Concentrate on visualizing happiness as a
ball of energy that flows through you and
from you to others you encounter in your life.
See your family, friends and colleagues as
glowing with happy energy which surrounds
and protects them.

189

Let your attention settle comfortably on one place in your body and breathe deeply for a while. Next, let your conscious awareness spread to fill your entire body from the top of your head down to your toes, so that you're like a spider sitting in the middle of a web – the spider is sitting in one spot, but it is sensitive to the entire web.

Keep your awareness expanded like this and think of your breath coming in and out of your entire body through every pore. Let your awareness stay there for a while. There's nowhere else you have to go, nothing else you have to think about. When you return gently from the meditation, you will feel focused and refreshed.

190

Meditation involves acceptance

All that is, has always been, and will always be.

Buddha, 560–480 BC

191

For physical regeneration and rejuvenation of the body

This is a way of aligning your body with the natural energy field of the Earth.

❖ Determine the precise direction of north by using a compass. Lie down with your head toward the south and your feet your pointing north. Relax your mind and your body by your breathing.

❖ Imagine your body sinking into the ground beneath you – feel the sensations. See yourself as being at one with the Earth. Deepen this visualization until you can actually feel yourself turning with the Earth. After five minutes reverse the position of your body so your head faces north and your feet south.

❖ Repeat the meditation. Continue for at least five minutes in each direction.

192

The importance of attitude to meditation

Your attitude reflects the value you place on something. When you start to meditate you will experience beneficial results. After a while, however, you may feel that you are not progressing sufficiently. It is important constantly to re-examine and relearn your meditation techniques in order to continue to experience beneficial results.

193

Think about how your actions affect others and never guard your honor at the expense of another.

194

Sit comfortably and concentrate on your
breathing. Move your awareness to the lower
right-hand corner of your abdomen and be
aware of your breathing there. Notice how it
feels as you breathe in, and how it feels as you
breathe out.

After five minutes do the same with the
lower, left side of your abdomen.

Then let your awareness spread out so that
it fills your entire body, like the light from a
candle in the middle of a room. Stay aware of
this light and feel how it encloses and protects
you.

Buddhist

195

The full lotus position

The most stable of all positions for meditating is the full lotus where each foot is placed up on the opposite thigh. This is perfectly symmetrical and very solid. Stability and efficiency are the important reasons why sitting cross-legged on the floor works so well. What is most important in Zazen meditation, though, is what you do with your mind and for this you must be sitting in a position that is comfortable for you.

196

Begin to focus

Find a simple object which is easy to visualize – an egg or a candle, for example. Hold the object you have found, look at it and close your eyes. Keep the image in your thoughts. Try to see it as if your eyes were open. When you are able to visualize your object for one minute, you are ready for your meditation.

197

Meditation for helping others

As you enter your meditative state, repeat the thought to yourself, "I must cherish all living beings because they are so kind to me". Through this meditation you will learn to cherish all living beings – you will develop the sense that all living beings are important and that their happiness matters. Try to focus your mind on this feeling and maintain it for as long as you can.

When you complete your meditation try to maintain your calm, loving mind so that whenever you meet or remember someone you naturally think: "This person is important, the happiness of this person matters".

198

Sit or lie down in a quiet place. Prepare to
meditate by breathing deeply and evenly.
Breathe in slowly to a count of four. Hold
your breath to a count of two. Then exhale
slowly.

As you continue to breathe deeply and
evenly, create a picture in your mind of you
doing something relaxing – walking
somewhere beautiful and peaceful, for
example. Allow yourself to recall the details of
the experience, remembering the sights, the
sounds, the smells, the feelings, and your
mood. Simply allow yourself to relive the
moment. Breathe deeply and evenly. Relax
and enjoy the memory.

199

Meditation checklist

Simply practising this checklist of how to get ready to meditate, without actually meditating, can make you feel calmer.

Keep your back straight to allow your diaphragm to move freely so that your breathing can be deep, easy, and natural. Keep your mouth closed – unless you have a nasal blockage of some kind – breathe through your nose. Press your tongue lightly against your upper palate.

Keep your eyes closed or lowered with your gaze resting on the ground about two or three feet in front of you. There should be no tension in your body. Your mind and breath should be one reality. When your mind is at rest your breath will be deep, easy, and effortless.

200

For a more relaxed outlook on life, keep paying attention to your breathing and at the same time try to develop your kindness and compassion towards others. Try constantly to release yourself from stress and tension and work ceaselessly on your personal relationships.

201

Flowing

Allow your body to move spontaneously with each breath. Don't attempt deliberate, choreographed movements – let your body stretch and move as it wishes.

202

Opening chakras

❖ Sit upright in a chair with both feet firmly on the floor and your hands on your legs.

❖ Inhale for five seconds, hold your breath for one second and then slowly exhale for five seconds. This will slow down your heart rate and help you to relax. Do this for three or four minutes.

❖ Starting with your base chakra (your groin area), as you inhale imagine a red sphere pulsating and getting brighter as the pulses become stronger. Keep that image clear within your mind.

❖ With the next inhalation picture the spleen chakra (under your ribs) beginning to glow while at the same time continuing to visualize the base chakra glowing below it. Exhale again. Keep on inhaling and exhaling, imagining each chakra (throat then forehead) pulsating and glowing. By the crown chakra (the top of your head) you should see all the globes glowing and pulsating down the front of your body.

❖ By now you should be well relaxed and

you will probably find as you carry on that
your breaths will become quite shallow.
This exercise is excellent for re-energizing
the body.

203

Standing meditation

Bend your knees and keep your feet firmly on
the ground. Hold your arms out in front of
you as if about to embrace someone. Relax
your shoulders and allow your body to sway if
it needs to. Concentrate on the idea of being
firmly connected to the Earth with deep
regular breaths. Feel centered and stronger
with each deep breath. Do this for five
minutes.

204

A simple meditation exercise

❖ Find a quiet place where you will not be disturbed and assume a comfortable position lying on your back or sitting. If you are sitting, keep your spine straight and let your shoulders drop.

❖ Close your eyes if this makes you feel more comfortable.

❖ Bring your attention to your abdomen, feel it rise or expand gently as you inhale, and fall or recede as you exhale. Focus on your breathing, "being with" each inhalation.

❖ Practise this exercise for 15 minutes at a convenient time every day. In time, this will give you the ability to concentrate for longer and to feel calmer under pressure.

205

Nada yoga meditation

Plug your ears with your thumbs and concentrate on your internal body sounds. At first the sounds will be faint, but they will become progressively louder. By listening to these sounds your mind will become internally focused. These sounds are a very beneficial meditative object and this meditation can be done anywhere – it is an especially good meditation to perform at work.

206

The repetition of a meditation sound has a harmonizing effect and induces relaxation and peace of mind as well as liberating new resources. If you use a meditation sound in your meditations you can induce a state of calm at any time of the day by closing your eyes and "hearing" that sound.

207

The enhanced relaxation exercise

This is a particularly good exercise to perform at bedtime. Lie down and take several deep breaths. Then breathe in slowly as you tense the muscles in your feet. Hold your breath and the tension for a count of ten or 20. Then, slowly breathe out, releasing the muscles until they are totally relaxed. Repeat the process with your calf muscles, and work your way up your body, finishing with your facial muscles. Finish with a few more deep breaths.

208

Thought-stopping technique

This technique involves stopping stressful thoughts before they have a negative effect on you. By isolating the stressful thought and silently saying "stop" you can release the thought from your mind. If the thought doesn't go away, simply repeat the process until it does.

209

Meditation for concentration

Sit comfortably on the floor or in a chair.
Keep your back straight but not strained. Keep
breathing slowly and deeply. Think of a
favorite object. In your mind, draw that object
as beautifully as you can. Think of its shape,
its design, its colour, its texture, its smell. If a
distracting thought comes into your mind,
notice the thought, but then bring your mind
back to your chosen object. Keep breathing
slowly and deeply.

Try to meditate on your object for five
minutes. If five minutes is easy, try ten or 20.
This exercise will help you to focus your mind.

210

A sequence for instant calming

❖ Practise uninterrupted breathing. When stress strikes, immediately focus on your breath and continue breathing smoothly, deeply and evenly.

❖ Balance your posture. People under stress often look hunched over.

❖ Bathe in a wave of relaxation. Consciously sweep a wave of relaxation through your body.

❖ Acknowledge reality. Face the causes of your stress head-on. Don't try to deny your stress or wish it away. In your mind feel the words: "This is real. I can handle it. I'm finding the best possible way to cope right now".

❖ Reassert control. Instead of fretting about how the person who has caused you stress has robbed you of control, focus on what you can control (your mind), and take appropriate action.

211

Sit comfortably with your spine straight and start your breathing exercises. As you breathe, call in light to your body. At first the light will not be very bright but perseverance with meditation will gradually but steadily increase the power of the light. Eventually the light will be pervasive – it will infuse every aspect of your personal life with brightness and happiness.

212

A dictionary definition of meditation is: "The act of meditating; close or continued thought; the revolving of a subject in the mind". In every meditation you practise you should be clear about its purpose and concentrate your energies appropriately. This will make the meditation more effective.

213

Love

❖ Make yourself comfortable in a chair with both feet on the ground.

❖ Take some deep, even breaths and use your breathing to relax your body and clear your mind.

❖ Imagine that there is a circle of light by your heart. This is the source of active love that is in everything you do. From here comes your ability to love and includes your ability to empathize, sympathize and forgive.

❖ As you breathe, concentrate on this energy and you will experience an overwhelming sense of fullness which is felt as love.

214

Movement meditation

Center your mind and concentrate. Take
several deep and cleansing breaths. Then move
into a relaxed, squatting stance with your
knees slightly bent and your hips and pelvis
loose.

Center yourself by visualizing your feet
connected to the soil. Visualize the center of
the Earth drawing energy up into you. Focus
your awareness. Gently move your body in an
undulating, snakelike, swaying motion. See
yourself as a flower opening up, as an animal
moving through the brush or a tree swaying in
the breeze.

Dance, if you like – use sound or music to
focus your attention on the movement and on
the vibration. Allow yourself to get lost in the
sense of movement. Feel the areas of your
body that are tight and let the movement
loosen them up.

215

You probably meditate already!

Often people meditate without even knowing
it. For example, when you daydream or find
your mind fixed on one thought, that is a
form of meditation. Watching the sunset or
listening to the wind rustle through the leaves
is often done in a meditative state – at that
moment the rest of the world around you
seems at a remove. The real key to meditation
is to be able to exercise control over your
thoughts and awareness of the world around
you.

216

The spirit rises mightier by defeat.

Sri Aurobindo (Savitri), 1872–1950

217

A "child-within" meditation to give you strength

Visualize yourself as a small child. See yourself as you are now, talking to the child you were, and who is within you always. Tell the child that in spite of all the fears that she or he had, everything has turned out all right because you are there now and everything is okay. Tell your child within that it's safe and never to worry again. You are now a responsible adult and will always act appropriately. There is no need any longer for the child to worry and suffer.

218

Find a daily time and place to meditate

Set aside one or two half-hours each day. Select a time when you are least pressured. Of course, it is essential to have a quiet, uninterrupted place, perhaps your room or a private spot outdoors. It is important that you are not disturbed by external factors such as noise or other people.

219

When you need to feel protected

Visualize yourself in a cocoon of white light. You
should surround yourself completely. See the
light as bright and warm. You may play with this
sphere of light making it bigger or smaller until it
feels right for you. Say to yourself, "I am
protected by this pure white light of all that is
good and truthful. I am surrounded by this pure
light which keeps out all unwanted and evil
influences." This generates an aura that protects
you from outside influences.

220

Who is the real self that you communicate with in meditation?

The real self is reached by understanding who
you are not:

❖ You are not your body.
❖ You are not your mind.
❖ You are not your emotions.

221

A meditation to help you sleep

As you are breathing, see yourself lying in warm sunlight. The light is pleasant to be in. Starting with the tips of your toes, feel the sun warming all of your body, slowly moving up into your legs, your torso, then into your arms and fingers. As you feel this warming, become more and more relaxed, going deeper and deeper into a calm and quiet place.

222

A quick relaxing meditation at work

Relax yourself in the way that prepares you best for meditation. Focus your attention on your breath. Observe and feel air come into your body, stay, and leave the body. As you inhale count one, as you exhale count two and so on. Try to do this to a count of 100. It might sound easy but it is actually quite hard and will take some practise until you manage it.

223

A healing meditation

❖ Sit comfortably with both feet on the floor
and concentrate on your breathing.

❖ Sink into comfort and relaxation by seeing
yourself by a sunny stream or lake.

❖ Feel all tension slip away and feel renewed
with energy that you know will begin to
heal you. As you heal yourself you can heal
all those who cross your path.

❖ The healing vision of sunshine and water is
yours whenever you want it to be. You can
come back to this space whenever you
want to, knowing that it is always available
to you.

224

Feeling safe

Sit in a comfortable chair and have a table
nearby. On the table put some objects or
photographs that remind you of places and
people that you love. You need to create a
private space for yourself where you can feel
an immediate sense of peace. Close your eyes
and focus on the people or places that give you
great happiness. With each inhalation, feel the
joy these give you, and with each exhalation
keep the feeling with you as the images recede.
Each time you need to feel stronger and safe
close your eyes, focus your breathing and
return to this space.

225

Sit in a quiet place and relax your mind. Be aware of your breaths as you inhale and exhale for the first few minutes. Imagine being in your favorite place in the world. Try to really feel this space using your imagination. Picture yourself in this place feeling love, peace, and ecstatic joy. You can do this for ten or 15 minutes or more if you like, but when you have finished just let your mind be still. Don't think about anything, but keep your mind at peace.

226

Flame meditation for energy

Concentrate on the flame at the tip of a candle. See the white, blue, red, orange and yellow areas of the flame. Observe the way the light changes as it radiates from the candle. Observe the never-ending movement. Feel the warmth. In your mind's eye know that this energy is within everything, everywhere and you are at one with it.

227

Get into a comfortable, alert position and withdraw within

Sit in a comfortable, relaxed position. Do not lie down as your head should be free to move in this meditation. Any sitting position is fine, even in a simple straight-backed chair. Then close your eyes (unless focusing on a visual object). Sit quietly for a minute or so, letting your body relax and your mind forget the external pressures on you. Withdraw within yourself. See yourself deep within your center: safe, protected and strong. Even if you do this for only five to ten minutes a day, it will improve your confidence.

228

Meditation for forgiveness to others

With each inhalation you should visualize
yourself being filled with loving, forgiving
energy.

Inhale slowly and deeply and see yourself as
being cleansed. Hold your breath for as long
as it feels comfortable and send the energy to
every cell in your body, from your toes to your
scalp. Exhale slowly and deeply while
visualizing every physical, mental, and
emotional impurity leaving your body. With
every forgiving and cleansing inhalation,
retention and exhalation, see yourself
becoming pure, glowing, whole and holy.

When you see yourself as pure, visualize
someone who needs your forgiveness and send
your compassionate, loving forgiveness to
them. Forgive them in your heart and forget
their aberration.

229

Let the mind go free and observe it

As you meditate, give up control – simply let
things happen. Thoughts, plans, memories,
and fantasies will enter your mind. You may
get lost in a thought for a little while and
that's okay. When the thoughts have passed,
return to your focus of awareness. The mind
should be left free, "on its own". Calmly
observe whatever comes into your awareness:
images, fantasies, emotions, concerns,
thoughts or solutions. If it is important, you
will remember it – no effort is necessary.
Always return to your focus and make no
demands on your mind. With practice,
distracting sensations, like an itch, will fade
away. Your ability to relax will gradually
increase.

230

Clearing your mind

One of the best techniques to use when you
find it impossible to clear your mind is to fill
it completely. Focus on any object or concept,
like a table, then think of everything you can
that relates to a table. Whatever you do, keep
referring back to the object of your
concentration. Reflect also on how the table,
or other object, relates to anything, or
everything, in the universe. What will happen
eventually is that you will find that everything
you can think about relates in some way to a
table, or whichever object you have chosen.
Long before you get through the first billion
things that relate to your object, your mind
will surrender, become tired and empty of its
own accord.

231

Visualization

In meditation visualization is a powerful tool
for manifesting your will or for recreating past
events to allow yourself to take back your
power and begin the healing process. For a
basic visualization meditation imagine yourself
going on a journey, perhaps flying or
swimming underwater. The spirit is free and
you are spirit, so you are free to go wherever
you wish.

232

A quick scan for tension

Check your body for physical tension. Make it
a habit to stop several times a day to scan your
body mentally for areas where you are tense.
Command them to relax. You will quickly
learn where you keep your tension and when
you command that area to relax, tension will
melt away from your whole body.

233

Using colors in meditation

Different colors are associated with different uses in meditation.

Red:
* Energizes the blood and the circulatory system, including the kidneys and liver
* Stimulates physical and emotional energy

Orange:
* Energizes the digestive system, pancreas and spleen
* Helps to create a positive mental outlook

Yellow:
* Energizes the digestive and elimination systems
* Helps to stimulate creativity and other mental processes
* Helps to create a positive outlook

Green:
* A powerful healing color
* A balancing color for the whole body

- ❖ Has a calming effect which can help with anxiety and the nervous system
- ❖ Helps to stimulate physical healing after trauma
- ❖ Should not be used with cancer or tumors as it promotes growth

Pink:
- ❖ A good overall balancing color
- ❖ Helps with anger and loneliness
- ❖ Helps to stimulate feelings of compassion

Blue:
- ❖ A cooling color
- ❖ Helps to balance and energize the respiratory system
- ❖ Helps with high blood pressure

Indigo:
- ❖ Works on a deep, intuitive level
- ❖ Helps with self-actualization and enlightenment
- ❖ Helps with healing from cancer and the effects of chemotherapy and radiotherapy

White:
- ❖ Can be used for protection and for attaining the upper levels of enlightenment

❧ Detoxifying and cleansing
❧ Can be used if you are unsure which color to use

Gold:
❧ A powerful healing color
❧ Helps with overall well-being and mental attitude
❧ Balances all aspects of being: physical, emotional and spiritual
❧ Helps to amplify the body's own healing resources, bringing them to bear wherever needed

234

If you want to meditate using colors but are finding visualization difficult, you can use colored cards to help see the color in your mind. Choose the color you want and concentrate on that color for about ten minutes. Repeat until you feel you have had enough.

235

A healthy cleansing exercise

❖ Position yourself in your most comfortable
meditation posture. Relax your body,
mind, and emotions. Inhale deeply for four
units of time. Fill your lungs completely,
so you can see and feel your abdomen
distend. Retain your breath for the count
of four and then exhale for the count of
eight. Any rhythm that you establish
naturally is the right one for you.

❖ When you inhale, visualize all healthy
qualities coming to you. See and feel
yourself inhaling purity, sweetness,
gentleness, health, vitality and calmness.

❖ Now exhale all impurities for a count of
eight. See and feel pain, anger, illness,
ignorance, impatience, and all negative
energies leave you.

❖ This meditation technique is specifically
designed as a healthy cleansing exercise.

236

Once you have found a quiet spot and have at least an hour to yourself, turn off the phone and any other sources of disruption. Imagine a wave of relaxation starting at your toes and flowing to every part of your body – including your arms, hands, shoulders, head, face and so on. Feel your body becoming heavy – this is a sign that you are relaxing. Now breathe in and out slowly and deeply, cleansing your body. Let all the tension leave your body with each exhalation. Feel more and more relaxed with every inhalation.

237

To feel peaceful and bring peace to others

As you enter your meditative state think:
I am a soul, distinct from my body.
I am emanating into the body.
My basic characteristic is peace.
Help me to discover it.

238

A simple meditation

Once your body is relaxed sit quietly. Do not think – just be. Slowly imagine a bright light form around you; the light is energy and love. Let it wash over your body, taking with it any aches or pains, emotional or physical. Let it linger for as long as it feels right. When you are ready, imagine the light becoming smaller and smaller, leaving you feeling lighter. When you complete your meditation you will be filled with energy and will feel good for the rest of the day.

239

Duration of meditations

You can meditate for as little as five minutes or for 45 minutes or longer, depending on the time available to you and the goal of your meditation. Ideally, though, you should meditate for at least 15 minutes once or twice a day.

240

Talking with guides

It is possible to receive guidance during meditation. You can ask to speak with your spirit guide. Once you have made contact with your spirit guide try to let the words flow into your mind without judgement. You will know they are the words of a guide from the feeling of love attached to them. Sometimes it is not words you will hear but scenes you will be shown, or music you will hear. There are many different forms of communication. For everyone it is different and there is no right or wrong way to communicate with a spirit guide.

241

Self-guided imagery

With self-guided imagery you can program yourself for any outcome you desire. You can set goals for yourself or help to heal yourself.

242

Visualizing color

Stand with your feet slightly apart and your
arms by your sides, relaxed with the palms
turned to the front. Relax your shoulders and
concentrate on your breathing. You could also
lie down or sit comfortably.

Visualize yourself in a place where you feel
safe and relaxed. This could be in a natural
setting with beautifully colored flowers, or
swimming in a blue sea or relaxing on a lovely
beach with white sand. Visualize a color you
want to work with and, staying conscious of
your breathing, absorb that color, holding
your breath in for a few moments while the
color fills your body. Then breathe out all the
stress, pain and turmoil. Repeat this three to
seven times.

243

Many people meditate at night before sleeping. Since meditation will take your body, brain and mind in the direction of sleep, getting too comfortable in your bed when meditating may result in you falling asleep. If your goal is to meditate before bedtime, then consider sitting up in your bed for the meditation part, and after meditating, get yourself more comfortable and drift into sleep. If your goal is to get to sleep, you will probably manage to do so faster and more easily through meditation. Imagining yourself in a safe place is often a good visualization technique for sleep.

244

Raise your hands to chest level facing outward. Release excess energy by blessing the Earth with light, loving kindness, peace and prosperity for several minutes until you feel your body is normalized and calmed. You may bless specific people or your family and friends after releasing the excess energy.

245

A quick way to clarify your mind

- ✤ Become aware of your breath at the nostrils.
- ✤ Notice how the air feels entering your nostrils.
- ✤ Notice how the air feels exiting your nostrils.
- ✤ Continue doing this for several minutes.
- ✤ As you become aware of each breath entering and exiting, begin counting each cycle.
- ✤ Continue doing this for approximately twenty minutes.
- ✤ Try to do this exercise on a daily basis to improve your awareness.

246

Goal-setting and problem-solving

As you enter your meditative state, visualize your present situation or problem, and then imagine the desired goal or solution. With practice you will have more confidence in yourself to achieve your best whatever you try.

247

Light a candle during your meditation. This will help to raise your energy and give you greater focus. As you begin, release all the tensions and anxieties of your day in order to approach your meditation fresh. Imagine a clear, white light pouring in through the top of your head and running through your body and out through your feet, taking all your tension with it. Let this continue until you feel clear and open.

248

As you enter your meditation you may begin to feel different physically. You may feel heavy or light. You may even have the sensation of floating. Often, during deep physical relaxation, you may experience a sense of desensitization, and feel as if your body is no longer there. This is actually a sign that your meditation is going well.

249

Four steps to meditating

❖ Entering. Every meditation begins with some kind of entry. Breathing is often the catalyst at this stage.

❖ Deepening. Once you have entered your meditation it is time to deepen. Deepening is done by relaxing your body and mind, often while counting breathing.

❖ Purpose. By the time you get to this stage your body is extremely relaxed, your brain frequency is slow, and your mental state is at its deepest and most receptive. This makes it ideal for any kinds of goal-setting, problem-solving techniques or the use of guided imagery.

❖ Exit. Coming out of a meditative state is as simple as opening your eyes. You can exit the meditation more gradually by counting slowly from one to three. Another way of exiting a meditation is by entering sleep.

250

The "deep breaths" method of meditating

❖ Get into a comfortable position, then close your eyes and take the first deep breath. Keep on breathing deeply and regularly.

❖ For good physical relaxation it is important to relax one part of your body at a time. This could be done head to toes or toes to head. You may take 15 minutes, 20 minutes, or even longer doing the part-by-part body relaxation.

❖ When you do this for the first time, first tense the muscles of your body tightly and then relax them bit by bit. This can help to establish a clear distinction between tension and relaxation and make it easier to learn to relax during the exercise and in the future.

251

Head-first relaxation

Concentrate on the skin covering your head.
Feel the skin that covers your scalp and then
relax and release all tensions and pressures
from your scalp and place them in a deep state
of relaxation. Taking your time, do the same
for the rest of your body. Remember to take
occasional deep breaths through your nose as
if filling your belly with air. Then breathe out,
exhaling through your nose. Breathe in this
way whenever you want to enter a more
relaxed state. When you reach full and deep
physical relaxation, make a strong mental
impression of the experience. Allow your
body, brain, and mind to memorize how it
feels to be deeply relaxed so that you can
create it quickly, and easily in future
meditations.

252

Sense the touch of your hands on your lap or your knees, or sense the points of contact of your legs, feet, and bottom against the cushion or the floor. Concentrate only on these bodily sensations – how do they feel? Gently allow any thoughts to pass over you and move away again.

Do this for five minutes or so in the morning to energize you for your day.

253

"Catch yourself" consciously throughout the day

During the day make several attempts to "catch yourself". Become aware of your thoughts, your feelings and your inner essence. Detach yourself – simply watch the "video" and let your thoughts pass as you witness yourself in your world.

254

An exercise for minimizing stress and struggle

As you inhale, gently shift your attention and your sense of identity to your inner spirit, your calm inner awareness beyond your body, mind, and emotions.

As you exhale, relax and let go, allowing the life energy to flow freely and naturally upward through your entire body.

Breathe normally, although your breathing might naturally deepen a bit.

This exercise can be practised whenever your attention is not fully engaged in an essential task, even when you are standing in the queue at the market.

255

To radiate calmness to others

As you enter your meditation, imagine an intensely bright, golden-white light shining deep within your heart. Think of it as a boundless inner reservoir of spiritual light. Now imagine this brilliant golden-white light gently radiating outward from your heart, beaming out in all directions.

Just breathe and let the light gently beam out from your heart.

After ten or 15 minutes, take a couple of deep breaths and slowly open your eyes.

256

Countdown deepening exercises

The quickest way to deepen your state of meditation at any point is to take a deep breath and say to yourself, "Deeper and deeper" or do a short countdown from ten to one, saying "Deeper and deeper" between numbers.

257

Meditate for peace

While meditating, extend your arms and imagine the Earth suspended and rotating between your two hands. Imagine projecting healing energy from your right hand to your left. Imagine this healing energy going right through and completely surrounding the Earth.

As you are doing this, think of all those who are involved in turmoil and suffering and with all your heart picture yourself emanating healing energy to the Earth suspended in space, rotating.

258

Close your eyes, and gently begin to inhale and exhale. Feel as if you are ridding yourself of all your negative energy, and being embellished by positive energy. Concentrate on your breathing, and try not to let your thoughts wander off. Picture a point in your mind – a simple dot in a white space. Concentrate on this dot and in your mind feel yourself embraced by love, happiness and tranquility.

259

To release tension caused by worries

Keep your neck straight and push upward
with the top of your head. In this way internal
energy is moving upward while at the same
time energy is also sinking to the lower
abdomen. When one is meditating correctly
without blockages this is how the energy flows
in the body. This is also how energy is created
– it is very important to keep the spine as
straight as possible.

260

Position of the body

As a beginner, it is important not to get too comfortable. Getting too comfortable while meditating can lead easily to sleep. In the beginning, a sitting position is best with your feet apart and flat on the floor, your spine as straight as possible, your head slightly lowered, and your hands on your lap, palms up or down, whichever feels more comfortable to you. Do not slouch and do not cross your legs, ankles, or arms. This may make you uncomfortable later on during the meditation, causing you to shift your focus away from the internal mental experience in order to tend to physical discomfort. With time and practice you will be able to meditate in any position you choose.

261

Meditation for your emotions

With your eyes closed, take a few moments to pay attention to your breathing. Next, try to focus your attention on the emotions you are feeling. Try not to analyze them, alter them, or push them away. Just feel them.

Now, imagine a radiant face, the face of the most loving, caring, compassionate being you can think of. Spend a few minutes communing with this loving being. Converse with the being if you like, mentally or aloud. Then offer up your negative emotions to this loving being for healing. Simply turn them over to be healed and transformed. When you are ready, slowly come out of your meditation.

262

Gathering the mind

As you focus on breathing you'll notice that various thoughts and emotions arise. When this happens, acknowledge that you are thinking and return your focus to the breath. As you continue to apply the technique of recognizing thoughts and returning your focus to the breath, the torrent of thoughts slows down to a river, then to a meandering stream, which eventually flows into a deep, calm ocean. Practise this any time during the day.

263

Keep a notebook of your intuitions

Capture dreams, insights and ideas that come to you without effort during meditation. Reread them after a few weeks and see how they related to what went on in your life and how your intuitive senses were communicating with you.

264

You can meditate on a simple walk to the shops. As you walk, notice your surroundings – the light, the smells and the sounds. Sometimes the most ordinary, everyday things can put you in a rapturous state if you really look at them or watch them. You might not have realized it but many of your walks have probably been meditative. When you open yourself to your environment, heighten your sensory awareness and experience deep joy and presence in the moment – that is meditation.

265

A very powerful way to ground your thoughts is to visualize colored cords of light connecting you to the Earth. Then visualize energy flowing out from the Earth up the cords, destroying them. Then visualize new colored cords. Repeat this process several times until you feel grounded and stable and connected to the Earth.

266

Find a quiet place and begin slow, circular breathing with pauses between exhaling and inhalation, breathe continuously and make sure the exhalation is completely relaxed in every way.

Next, feel all the sensations in your body. Pay attention to whatever is the strongest feeling in that moment. As each moment comes and goes, the strongest feeling is likely to change. Move your attention to follow it. Imagine that you are pulling each inhalation in through that strongest feeling.

267

For calmer days

Sit on a chair, feet on the ground, spine erect, hands clasped and eyes closed. Take five deep breaths and begin to focus on the rhythm of your breathing. Say "In" as you inhale and "Out" as you exhale. If you become distracted, just return to your focus as soon as possible. This meditation will eventually calm your mental body and your work will benefit.

268

Meditation to balance your physical body

Sit comfortably and begin by breathing deeply. Concentrate in your mind on the various muscles in your body, starting with your feet and moving up to the top of your head. Feel them warming as if you were doing physical exercise. Gradually feel your whole body becoming warmer and more relaxed. Repeat this four or five times until you feel relaxed in body and mind.

269

Drinking water and meditation

Drink lots of water. As you grow spiritually and evolve through meditation, you begin to release toxins and your body becomes and feels more energetic. It is very important to drink lots of water to make sure this heightened amount of energy can flow easily throughout your body.

270

When you first start meditating, silently
confirm your experience of being in the now.
"Now I am going to meditate. Now I am
closing my eyes. Now I am breathing deeply.
Now I am visualizing the colour blue".

As you progress in your practice, staying in
the present will become second nature, and
saying it to yourself will no longer be
necessary. Initially, though, it is important to
be fully aware of how it feels to be totally
immersed in the moment. Being able to
concentrate only on the present is a beautiful
experience and the best way to ensure
complete relaxation of your mind.

271

Sit with your eyes closed and breathe deeply
until you feel more relaxed. Repeat to yourself:
I am the light, I am the strength, I can
accomplish anything.

Repeat this at least ten times until you feel
more centered. Have patience in your practice.
You will become better at meditating with
more experience.

272

Issues during meditation

It is possible to meditate on issues and problems directly affecting daily life. Care must be taken to ensure that if you use a problem or an issue, you adopt a detached attitude or phrase the issue in such a way as to be as impersonal as possible. It would be best to have some practise at meditation before attempting to use personal problems as a focus.

273

The best time to try an energy healing meditation is just before bedtime. Sleeping after meditation integrates your mind's healing energy with your body. This allows the body to integrate the experience as quickly as possible. Having a strong intent to accept the healing and to let go of the past also helps. After energy healing meditation your body will be detoxifying. It is very important that you drink lots of water to help your body to flush out the toxins that are released.

274

Atonement

You can do therapeutic work, or have a large network of people for support, but still not feel forgiven. That sort of forgiveness comes from a place of surrender. While you meditate, offer your good intentions, loving thoughts and kind wishes. Surrender your mind to the cleansing effects of pure consciousness and you will soon feel the lightness in your heart on a daily basis.

275

Use short intuitive exercises

Teach yourself how to get a quick yes/no answer. Visualize an internal sign or meter that you can see clearly as yes or no. It can be done with color or with a more literal image of a clock or dial. Practise testing it with clear yes and clear no questions. Then ask questions with unknown answers. When you become good at this then you can use it accurately even in a pressured situation.

276

Energy healing meditation to balance your emotions

Emotions have a very short life span. They are meant to flow through us and then out of us, not to be held within us. What often happens, though, is that we feel an emotion and get caught up in it and it stops the flow. By breathing deeply into your heart while you experience the feeling, you can allow the emotion to flow through you and leave. Allowing yourself to let go of these emotions is cleansing to your body and mind.

277

Learn to focus for quick meditation

You can use repetitive movements to still the mind – doing it this way you can even meditate while walking on a treadmill, or while sitting and knitting for example. Concentrate only on the repetition and clear your mind.

278

Meditation to balance your soul

Spend five minutes each morning before work, five minutes after work and five minutes before you go to bed saying out loud with sincerity: "I am love. I am whole. I am goodness. I am strength. I am me". This will make a big difference. Meditation may be walking in nature, swimming laps or immersing yourself in music. There are many ways to meditate but the key thing is to get into a state of consciousness where you are able to still your mind. It takes a while to do this so work up to it in small doses. Stilling your mind for two minutes is a good start for someone who has never meditated before.

279

Balancing your body, heart, mind and soul

In this meditation, focus on love because love heals the body, soothes the emotions, slows down the mind and helps the soul to develop. As you meditate, concentrate on healing the body with loving energy, then work with emotions, then the mind, then the soul and finally back to the body. Repeat the cycle.

280

Energy healing meditation for grounding

One of the quickest and easiest ways to ground your energy is to close your eyes and take ten deep breaths. Visualize your favorite tree. Pretend that you are that tree and visualize your arms being branches. Anchor your feet firmly on the ground and visualize thousands of roots extending deeply into the earth. This is a great exercise to do whenever your energy feels really scattered or you feel spacey.

281

Freedom from guilt

When you begin to meditate, make a
commitment to continue for three months.
Set aside ten to fifteen minutes each day, and
choose a comfortable place for your
meditation. Take seven to ten deep breaths,
and allow the feeling of guilt to come to mind.
Try to work out where your feel it in your
body – your neck, your shoulders, your heart.
The key result is that you will begin to realize
that you are not the feeling, you're having the
feeling.

282

Put your hand on your stomach in the center just below your ribcage. Breathe in deeply through your nose, and fill this area with air first, feeling your abdomen expand. Fill your lungs from the bottom up and release this breath through your mouth, slowly.

It is generally best to exhale for twice as long as your inhale breath, but you will do that naturally most of the time. Do this daily for ten minutes to start with for at least three weeks.

283

Try a "moving" meditation

Stand up and stretch your arms up as high as you can, and put your head all the way back so you are looking up. Slowly come all the way down and allow your body to relax totally. Your hands should be brushing the floor (don't push it if they don't) and allow your head to simply hang.

Now slowly, bring yourself back to the first position, and then hold it for a time, and slowly bring yourself to the second position, and hold it for a time. Continue to do this until you feel you've done enough. Then slowly come out of the meditation and sit down and rest.

284

Mental meditation

If your mind interprets a situation as stressful
(threatening, irritating, sad, etc.), it signals
your emotional body, triggering a related
emotional response: fear/anxiety,
anger/impatience, sadness/depression.

By clearing your mind, meditation helps
you to view your circumstances more "truly".
With this greater clarity, the mind begins to
interpret fewer situations as "stressful", and so
becomes less inclined to send unnecessary
emotion-triggering signals to your emotional
body.

285

Quieting the emotional body

In meditation, water is often a symbol for the emotions. As you meditate, visualize a stormy sea and then, very slowly, visualize the storm ending and the waters becoming calm. If visualization is difficult, act as if you are doing it yourself. If you cannot manage to calm the sea, your emotions are not sufficiently silent. In that case, don't go any further. Instead imagine walking into the sea with the bright, warm sun taking you in its rays, and let the warmth nurture and soothe you until you are ready to either walk out or feel ready to visualize a calm body of water.

286

Quieting the mind

To do this you need to let go of everyday cares
and thoughts. Visualize a mountain that you
carefully climb, aware that each step will take
you away from the everyday world. In the
beginning you may find climbing this
symbolic mountain a bit arduous, but it will
eventually become easier and you then need to
make sure you go slowly so that the quieting
of the mind can actually take place. On top of
the mountain is a garden. You may picture it
as manicured or as wild as you wish.
Somewhere in that garden there is a spot
uniquely reserved for you. It is a very beautiful
place, walk there and sit whenever you need to
feel more calm.

287

It is useful to have a thought to contemplate while you meditate to gain deeper concentration. An example might be, "Love surrounds us, but only one who loves can direct its current".

The deeper the connection with your mind is, the clearer and the more accurate your meditation will be.

288

Energy healing meditation to balance your mind

A great exercise is to buy a small notebook you can keep in a pocket or bag and write down everything you say out loud about yourself. If you do this conscientiously for even a week, you will become aware of what your negative mental patterns are. The first step to healing your mind is to understand your thought patterns and belief systems. In this way when you visualize the healing light energy your mind is receptive to its needs.

289

Silencing the mind

As a means to learn how to deal with unwanted thoughts, it is helpful to be the Observer, the one who looks on, who sees and knows but is not attached. As such you can quickly learn to see thoughts come and go. Visualize a basket into which unhelpful thoughts can be discarded. Or you could visualize a hand gently taking those thoughts away. In time, with practice, the activity of the mind decreases greatly.

290

Meditating on the meditation

Sit in a chair, eyes open, take as long as you
need to anchor within yourself what happened
during the meditation, a sort of debriefing.
Often there is a discrepancy between the
recollection and the meditation itself. The task
is to work inwardly with the thoughts, the
words and images until you sense that point of
peace allowing you to know your
understanding is at one with the event.

When you feel you have taken this
integration as far as it can go, the meditation
is over.

291

Seed thoughts

In meditation, you need to learn to penetrate your inner world and make it meaningful. A very good way to do this is through the use of seed thoughts. Although they appear to have one meaning on the surface, good seed thoughts grow, and as they do, they unmask hidden meanings. What enables us to discover these hidden layers is our contact with this hidden world. You should use the same seed thought several times before going on to another.

In keeping with focusing on the meaning of the inner and the outer within us the following seed thought is a step in that process:

"Having pervaded the universe with a fragment of myself, I remain."

From the Bhagavad Gita

292

The two types of meditation

❖ Analytical meditation. When we
contemplate the meaning of a Dharma
instruction that we have heard or read we
are doing analytical meditation. By deeply
contemplating the instruction, eventually
we reach a conclusion or cause a specific
virtuous state of mind to arise. Analytical
meditation is often called simply
"contemplation".

❖ Placement meditation. Having found our
object through analytical meditation, we
then concentrate on it single-mindedly for
as long as possible to become deeply
acquainted with it. This single-minded
concentration is placement meditation.

293

Allowing a "half-smile" as you meditate relaxes
the muscles in your face and affects your inner
and outer demeanor as well.

294

Imagery in preparation and rehearsal

Visualization can allow you to practise in advance for a future event, so that you are prepared and already practised in handling it. This helps to give you the self-confidence you need to do something well.

Many athletes and performers use this method. Recently, a professional golfer admitted that he imagined himself playing a particular hole in a tournament before he actually played. In his mind he envisioned the ball going into the hole even before he putted. It worked and he won the tournament.

295

Some people find that soft music and/or gentle incense help to create a meditative atmosphere. If you put on a calming track of music and enhance your senses with some fragrant incense or a candle, you may find relaxation easier.

296

Sit in a comfortable straight-backed chair, if you are able. Notice your breathing. Think "I am breathing in" and "I am breathing out." Breathing is pretty miraculous when we stop and think about it. After a few cleansing deep breaths, breathe naturally. Notice each part of your body, and how it feels as it is held in the chair. Focus your breathing for a time on any part of your body that is especially tense or painful to allow further relaxation. Return to your breathing and let a word or phrase come into your consciousness. This word or phrase will help you stay centered.

297

Energy healing meditation techniques

Find a peaceful place outdoors, lie down on the grass and look at the clouds roll by. This is a simple and very grounding practice. Children do it all of the time. You can easily find yourself in a meditative state while watching the clouds float across the sky.

298

In India many people sit on the beach watching the sunset. Listening to the sound of the waves, the seagulls, the wind and all the other sounds of nature around them. They bring their mind to peace by opening it up for relaxation. They call this meditation.

In the West meditation is better known in another context: the use of a mantra or a visualization technique. These meditations involve sitting calmly in a chair with eyes closed.

299

The process of undoing bewilderment is based on cultivating the ability to become familiar with our minds and strengthening them. Being observant and aware of what is happening in our minds gives us an opportunity to see a more profound level of truth all the time. In the practice of meditation, we learn to zoom back and get a bigger perspective, rather than always thinking small.

300

* Sit comfortably on the floor or in a chair.
* Close your eyes. Relax your body.
  Concentrate on your breath and feel the
  rhythm of life inside you. Think of
  nothing but the quiet breath in and out
  through your nose.
* Don't hurry your breath. Let it go
  naturally and softly just like your body
  wants it to.
* Repeat to yourself, "Stress is leaving me,
  peace is enveloping me".
* Let go of your other thoughts – think of
  your breath only.
* Feel the relaxation in your mind and the
  rhythm of your body.
* Sit like this for 20 to 30 minutes.

301

Make yourself physically comfortable. Sit erect, with your back straight, your feet planted firmly on the floor, your hands relaxed in your lap, breathing normally. Take a breath and count to four. Breathe in and out four or five times, counting, to quieten your mind.

Next, repeat silently or audibly, "I turn within to my own being". Sit quietly and ask, "Speak, my guide, and answer my problems".

Assume a listening attitude as if you were waiting to hear the answer. Many thoughts, ideas and answers will come to you. Trust your instincts and you will find the answer you are searching for.

302

Meditate for 15 minutes a day

The simplest way to meditate is to watch your breath. See the inhalation and see the exhalation. Imagine inhaling pure essence and exhaling all the bad air, negativity and worry of your day.

303

Walking meditation is liberating, and when it's done outdoors it connects you with nature. As you walk, you have the freedom to turn your attention outward as well as inward. Outward attention is when you concentrate on being part of the whole environment. You see colors and notice the movement of branches and leaves in the wind. You smell the fragrances of the earth; you feel the air on your skin.

To turn your attention inward, gaze down, just slightly ahead of your feet. Feel your breath, become conscious of your body's movement, and listen to your thoughts and emotions.

304

A walking meditation

Allow yourself at least 15 to 20 minutes to walk. However, even five or ten minutes can renew your spirit and energy.

1. Pause for a minute before you start, and feel yourself in the present. Notice your breath, then take several slow, deep breaths to increase your awareness.

2. As you begin, feel your feet connect with the ground. Isolate the sensation in your heels, toes and ankles. Feel the motion throughout your body, not just in your legs.

3. Breathe in through your nose and out through either your nose or mouth. Pay attention to the rhythm and flow of your breath.

4. Shift your attention from inward to outward, alternating between following the breath and focusing on the world around you. Devise a cycle that suits you, perhaps spending a minute on each, then switching.

5. Open up your senses. Feel the air as it moves across your skin; enjoy the quality of light. See the colours of flowers and trees. What sounds are you hearing? Observe the outer world as you would a painting, with heightened awareness.

6. At the end of your walk, pause, experience yourself again within your environment and listen to how you're feeling.

305

As you sit down to meditate, remind yourself
that you control your mind. Thoughts will
come and go endlessly. Ignore them. Go about
your business of concentrating on your
breathing or your contemplative meditation.
After you have been meditating for a while,
and your practice is well established, your
response will be one of amused tolerance as
you watch your wayward thoughts scurry
across the screen of your mind and disappear.

306

Out beyond ideas of
Right-doing and wrong-doing,
There is a field.
I'll meet you there.

Jelauddin Rumi, 1207–73

307

Take note of intuitive facts before making decisions

We all have certain ways of getting information, solving problems, thinking and acting. Next time you have to make a decision, turn your attention within and notice what your intuition is telling you. This will be beyond any fact. Notice if there is unresolved energy. You may need to ask more questions, clarify another person's intention, or change your approach. Also look at potential paths to take. Good ones fill you with energy and power, bad ones bring doubts and weakness.

308

Light meditation

This meditation helps you to reach deeper
levels of relaxation throughout your body.
Begin by imagining yourself surrounded by a
stream of beautiful light Slowly, this light
begins embracing your feet. It fills them with
rejuvenation and vitality. The light continues
up to your ankles, eradicating all pain and
expunging all negative energy. It continues to
your calves, your knees, your thighs and hips.
The light makes its way into your chest and
middle back. You are feeling very peaceful and
protected. The light continues throughout
your body. You are now completely embraced
in light, and have become part of the energy of
creation. The light is always with you, and
always there to give you comfort and relief
from distress.

309

Color meditation

As you relax through your breathing, begin to imagine an array of beautiful colors surrounding you. Try matching your spiritual needs with the symbolism of each color.

- ❖ blue – relaxation, quietude, calmness
- ❖ red – passion, excitement, emotions
- ❖ purple – intuition, psychic aptitudes, devotion
- ❖ pink – love, affection, compassion
- ❖ yellow – enthusiasm, happiness, joy
- ❖ orange – inspiration, creativity
- ❖ white – innocence, purity
- ❖ green – intelligence, wit, nature

310

Inner room meditation

Imagine yourself travelling through a tunnel of
light. At the end of this tunnel is a beautiful
room. This room could be anywhere.
Decorate this room however you want. Once
you have established your inner room, you can
begin your quest for self-knowledge. If you
simply want to get away from the troubles of
the world, just imagine yourself enjoying your
room and its surroundings. You have created
an inner sanctum that is impregnable to the
outside world. You can return to this place
whenever you want to.

311

Mantra meditation

Mantras are specific words that symbolize the divine energy of life. They can be powerful tools for achieving concentration. One of the most common mantras, is "om", which represents the harmony of unity, and of being at one with the universe. You can use any other word that you believe will give you strength, such as "love", "peace" or "harmony". Feel these words encompass your body and intertwine you with their meaning.

312

Sit comfortably and relax any tensions,
particularly in your face, neck and hands.
Allow your eyelids to close. Investigate how
you are feeling. Are you expectant or tense?
Then relax your attention a little.

Cultivate a spirit of enquiry in your
meditation. Take your time. Move your
attention, for example, systematically from the
crown of the head down over the whole body.
Notice the different sensations such as
warmth, pulsing, numbness, and sensitivity.
Ask how you are feeling in every part of your
body. This will enable you to become fully
relaxed into your meditative state.

313

In the words of the Buddha, the way is simple:
do good, refrain from doing evil, and purify
the mind.

314

Measure off about 25 to 30 paces of ground as
your meditation path. Stand at one end of the
path, and concentrate your mind on the
sensations of your body. First, let your
attention rest on the feeling of your body
standing upright, with your arms hanging
naturally and your hands lightly clasped in
front or behind.

Allow your eyes to gaze at a point about
three meters in front of you on the ground.
Now, walk gently, at a deliberate but normal
pace, to the end of the path. Stop. Focus on
your body standing for the period of a couple
of breaths. Turn, and walk back again. While
walking, be aware of the general flow of
physical sensations, or more closely direct your
attention to the feet.

315

After calming your mind, consciously put aside the meditation object. Observe the flow of mental images and sensations just as they arise, without engaging in criticism or praise. Notice any aversion and fascination; contemplate any uncertainty, happiness, restlessness or tranquillity as it arises and just be, meditating in the moment.

316

For this, you need an object to hold, like a stone or a lucky charm. Take your object and hold it in your hand. Now clear your mind. Don't think about anything in particular, and whatever thoughts may come to you need not be held on to or reacted to – rather let them drift right on through your mind. Meditate in this way for five to 15 minutes a day. When you finish, concentrate your energy out of the object you hold and give thanks.

317

Being receptive

If your meditation involves too much effort or control, it tends to spoil the spontaneous flow of grace. You can see this simple principle at work in the outer world as well. If you believe that you have to accomplish everything yourself, and never allow anyone to help, then of course no one will. So it is helpful to be receptive, and to approach meditation with the attitude of it being a combined venture, rather than a solo effort.

318

Stay in your calm centre

As often as possible throughout the day, try to remember to return to your calm inner centre that you reach in meditation. Being attentive to your breathing in between tasks, or when you are getting stressed, is one effective method for this.

319

Meditating on self-love

Sit comfortably and close your eyes. Now begin
to observe your personality. Notice your
thoughts, your emotions and how your body
feels.

Take some time to get acquainted with your
personality. Objectively, think about its
various characteristics. Next, imagine that your
personality is your child, and that you are its
parent.

Open your heart and embrace this child
with complete, unconditional love. This is a
simple meditation for learning to accept and
appreciate yourself just as you are.

320

Quieting the physical body

Begin by settling in a chair and loosening any
clothing that may be too tight. Take a few
breaths, as deep as you can make them and
exhale as slowly as possible. You may also use
any relaxation technique you are familiar with
or breathing exercises that you already know.
When you feel relaxed and at ease, close your
eyes and become aware of the weight of your
feet on the floor and of your arms on the
chair. Stay like this for up to 15 minutes
consciously relaxing your arms and legs.

321

Focus on your internal energy not your external tensions

When you sit down, assume a balanced posture to allow the energy in the centre of your body to move freely. If you're on a cushion, sit with your legs loosely crossed. If you're in a chair, keep your legs uncrossed and your feet flat on the floor. Imagine that a string attached to the top of your head is pulling you upright. Let your body settle around your erect spine. Place your hands on your thighs. The fingers are close and relaxed.

Tuck your chin in and relax your jaw. The tongue is also relaxed, resting against your upper teeth. Your mouth is ever so slightly open. Your gaze is downward or your eyes are closed. You aren't listening, but you do hear. Listen to your internal rhythm and count to slow it down to release tension from your body.

During this meditation you're not focusing with your senses but with your consciousness.

322

Inviting higher guidance

Imagine yourself in a place where you feel completely comfortable and at peace. Picture a being of light approaching from a distance. You can see that this being is radiating great peace, love, and wisdom. As he or she reaches you, you see that it is your higher self. Invite your higher self to sit with you. Briefly explain the situation and ask for his or her guidance. Your higher self may give you an answer in the form of words, symbols, pictures, or just a deep knowing. The answer may be very specific, or it may come in the form of a higher truth, which sheds enough light on the situation to help you choose wisely.

323

Some formal, step-by-step technique during meditation can be useful to a beginner. For example, a visualization process or a system of relaxing using breathing can help to focus the mind.

324

Breathing reminder

Be aware of your breathing and become accustomed to breathing deeply and rhythmically throughout the entire meditation. Take occasional deep breaths as you need for further deepening. Deep breaths will help relax your muscles, send oxygen throughout your body and brain, and slow down your pace. Occasional deep breaths will help keep you in a deep state of relaxation.

You have achieved deep breathing when you notice your belly rising and lowering with each breath. This is the type of breathing you normally experience when you are lying down.

325

As a man wishes in his heart, so he is.

Buddha, 560–480 BC

326

Progressive relaxation

Start by making a fist of each hand and holding it as tightly as you can. Then let go completely. Open your hands and see how different they feel. Move up to the forearms, tense them, then relax them. Now tense and relax the elbows, shoulders, neck, head, jaw, face, eyes, forehead and scalp. Next, work the upper back and chest in the same way, then start at the feet and move up the legs to the hips, concentrating on the genital area as you clench your muscles and then release them. Finally, tighten the whole body, hold your breath, and then suddenly let go. You should feel deeply relaxed at the end of this meditation.

327

Affirmations

An affirmation is a positive assertion you make to yourself about a goal during a meditation session. It can be a statement involving the things you want to have, do or be. It should be repeated often, both when awake and during meditation. Affirmations will make deep roots inside you when repeated in this way.

328

Meditation is a way of learning to relax your body while still keeping your mind alert. You may have felt this way when going for a walk in a park or forest, or along a beach, or after swimming, or during some other exercise.

You may have noticed it while watching a really good film, or being absorbed in a book or listening to your favourite music.

Normally, we go in and out of this calm, relaxed state many times during the day. All these things can be meditative.

329

Imagine that your mind is emitting electrical waves. As you slow down your mind, these waves become smaller, smoother and calmer. These energy waves are your thoughts. See and feel them calming until the waves are flowing peacefully.

330

A wandering mind

When meditating it is common for your mind to wander. This is normal. When you find your mind wandering, simply bring your attention back to whatever you are doing and continue where you left off. Occasionally, you may lose awareness and even enter sleep. This too is normal. With practice, this will happen less and less. Although concentration and focus will be enhanced through time, your mind's wandering nature will never go away completely.

331

To heal yourself

Once your body is relaxed, sit quietly. Picture yourself bathed in healing light energy. It is flowing from your head down through your body and out through your fingers and toes. You can mentally colour this energy whichever color is most suited to you at that time, whatever your body needs for healing and protection. Sit and feel peace for as long as you feel you can.

332

Sit comfortably with your back straight and your hands turned upwards, resting on your lap. Imagine a brilliant white or golden light on the crown of your head. Be aware for a few minutes of the light, the inner stillness and the bliss. Be aware of them and then let them go. Continue for about ten minutes. Let the light clear out all excess energy, taking it away as it runs through your body and out through your feet.

333

As you enter your meditation become aware of your heart and, with it, bless the entire Earth: every person, every being. Bless them with loving kindness, great joy, happiness, divine peace, understanding, harmony, good will and the will to do good. You may visualize the Earth as very small in front of you – raise your hands to chest level facing outward and feel the love flowing from your heart to your hands and enveloping the small Earth in front of you.

334

Exercise for after meditation

Shake the whole body 30 times, massage all the different body parts, then do physical exercises for a few minutes. This will greatly enhance the relaxation effect after you return from your meditative state.

335

When to practise

Mornings are the best time to meditate since your brain is more alert. All you need to do is close your eyes, take a deep breath, and enter your meditation.

Another good time to meditate is some time after lunch. If you have the time to meditate early in the afternoon, then this is a great time for long and deep meditations. We all have a natural tendency to feel a bit sluggish during the early afternoon hours, and meditation can serve to energize you and allow you to catch up with needed rest.

336

If you find yourself in a difficult situation where there isn't enough time to meditate using a traditional method, you can simply lower your eyes to the ground and breathe in slowly to the count of six then exhale to the count of six. If you think of nothing but breathing this can be a great way for instant relaxation.

337

Light a candle before you begin, for added energy. Clear away all tensions with a white light visualization. Then sit or lie comfortably. Imagine yourself in a beautiful, safe place. Imagine that your spirit guide is there with you, just like another person might be. Talk to them, and ask for any help that you may need, or assistance with any work that you'd like to do. Then clear your mind and listen. Sometimes the guide may answer right then. If this happens, feel free to have a dialogue with them; sometimes the answer will come to you later, or in the next few days.

338

One of the main objectives in meditation is simply to remain conscious. Another objective is to extend your consciousness into the slower frequencies where your mind stops racing and you are extremely calm. This will begin to happen even with only a moderate amount of practice.

339

To get rid of negative energy quickly

Close your eyes and enter a meditative state through a breathing or visualization exercise. See ahead of you in the distance a black hole. Force all your negative thoughts of the day into this black hole. Watch as the thoughts flow out of you and away through the black hole. When you have finished getting rid of your negative energy see the hole become smaller and disappear. In its place a bright light of positive energy begins to glow. When you feel cleansed you can return to the real world.

340

Expand your consciousness

❖ Begin by getting into a comfortable position.

❖ Place your awareness into the soles of your feet.

❖ Become aware of your feet.

❖ What do your feet feel like?

❖ Notice any different sensations in the various parts of your body.

❖ Slowly expand this awareness throughout your body.

❖ Only expand your awareness as far as you can without losing your awareness in the parts of your body you have already covered.

❖ If you perform this exercise daily, you will be able to expand your awareness further each time.

341

Quick walking meditation exercise

✤ Start by maintaining a good, straight, standing posture.

✤ Let your arms hang naturally. Clasp your hands in front or behind you.

✤ Allow your eyes to focus on a spot at ground level about five yards away. This helps to limit visual distractions.

✤ Focus your attention in the soles of your feet.

✤ Begin walking at a natural pace. This can be done in a car park or office environment – very useful when you get stressed at work.

342

You can meditate by sipping spring water. Close your eyes and concentrate on sipping water. Taste and feel each sip as it is in your mouth and as it travels down your throat. Think of nothing but the water. Do this at your desk or anywhere you feel the need to relieve tension.

343

Visualizing healing meditation

In your mind's eye, see aberrant or inflamed cells changing into healthy cells. If there is a damaged or corrupted area within the cells, visualize them changing and becoming free from injury. See your whole body becoming pure. Visualize yourself as perfectly healthy. Visualize healing energy filling you.

If you are suffering from pain, see in your mind's eye the nerve endings that are in the specific area of your discomfort. With every inhalation, feel and visualize healing air flowing from a higher power, entering you and filling your lungs. See your red blood cells absorb the air through the walls of your lungs and flow through your arteries spreading healing oxygen to every cell in your body. Witness the inflamed nerve endings become soothed and witness your body start to glow with well-being and serenity.

344

For energy

Visualize your body filled with life-giving
light. Witness your body energized. Visualize
each cell in your body filled with life-giving
light. Witness your cells energized. This same
energy is within every living thing, within all
things that walk the earth, that swim in the
water or fly through the air. It is within
everything that grows and everything that
lives. And it has a wisdom that directs all
activity. Visualize the infinite nature of this
life-giving light. This process of energy change
and exchange has been going on forever and
proceeds within you and without you now.
Merge with it and live happily ever after.

345

The end-of-guilt meditation technique

Sit in the position of comfort that you have come to know is best for maintaining meditation. Relax your mind, body, and emotions. Attain a rhythm of effortless breathing. Visualize yourself covered with many, many layers of ultra-fine energy, much like the layers of skin on an onion. Each of these layers can be seen as guilt. Realize that with every breath your spirit sends you forgiveness and blessings. Visualize your guilt coatings melting off and forgiveness cleansing and healing the wounds and pain they caused. As they peel off, you may remember specific things that you have been carrying within your subconscious. Witness the events and the suffering they represent fade away and dissolve forever.

346

Remember to draw in positive energy throughout the day

Say an affirmation several times a day, something simple like, "Spirit, guide, protect, and bless me" or, "I receive and fill with wisdom and love with every breath". This will continue to produce uplifting physical, mental, and emotional changes.

347

Record the experience

Some people find it useful to keep a diary of the experiences they have while they are in meditation. Or you could rate the relaxation and/or useful insight after each session in order to measure progress. Do not expect fantastic insights immediately. Understanding ourselves takes time. Eventually your diary entries will show you how much you have improved.

348

Basic astral technique

After entering into a meditative, relaxed state, visualize yourself sitting or lying down in whatever position you are in. Visualize your astral (spirit) body getting up and leaving your physical body and floating to a position approximately ten feet above your physical body.

Float up through the ceiling of the room you are in or right up in the sky. When you are about 100 feet in the air, look down and see the area you were just in. Think of somewhere on Earth and let yourself be pulled there. Look around. Be conscious of your surroundings without commenting, comparing, or judging. Let your awareness be pulled back to high above where you started. Look down at your physical body, and let yourself be pulled back into it.

349

Quick stress buster

Go somewhere quiet and lie down or sit in a chair with good back support so that your body is straight, allowing you to breathe deeply and comfortably. Tell yourself to relax. Work on every part of your body from the top of your head to your toes, consciously relaxing each part. Concentrate on your breathing, taking deep breaths through the nose when inhaling, letting the breath fill your body, relaxing and calming. Then breathe out through your mouth, exhaling all negativity and stress and ridding your body of the toxins that build up there. Repeat this a number of times even if you can only manage ten minutes.

350

Melt into your most comfortable meditative
posture. Visualize your grandparents being
born, see the events that take place in their
lives and see them eventually give birth to
your parents. Visualize events in your parents'
lives including your birth. As clearly as
possible, without reacting physically,
emotionally, or mentally, allow the movie of
the events of your life to unfold on the inner
screen of your mind's eye. Witness the events
in as detached a way as possible. By visualizing
the passage of time in this way, feel connected
to the cycles of the Earth.

351

Melt away tension

❧ Relax. With each exhalation send out a characteristic that has caused you to be blind to your light. With each inhalation bring into your being a divine attribute and feel yourself being purified. Send this energy throughout your body, mind, and emotions.

❧ Exhale fear; inhale courage.

❧ Exhale cold-heartedness; inhale compassion.

❧ Exhale ignorance; inhale wisdom.

❧ Exhale egoism; inhale humility.

❧ Exhale nervousness; inhale serenity.

❧ Exhale hate; inhale love.

❧ Exhale suffering; inhale peace.

❧ Continue until you have nothing else blocking your glory.

352

Flame meditation

Place a lit candle on the floor, about three to
six feet in front of you. It should be
somewhere your gaze falls on naturally
downward, or in front of you at eye level.
Simply focus on the flame. After gazing
steadily at the flame with eyes open, close your
eyes and visualize the flame. Send your
negative characteristics to the flame and see
them dissolve, burn away, or turn to ashes.
Dissolve all the things that take your peace
away. In your mind's eye, see yourself
becoming purer and purer as the flame grows
brighter with each offering.

353

Coming back to the real world after meditation

After 20 to 30 minutes in your meditative state, stop focusing your awareness (if visualizing), and allow yourself to slowly come out of the deep state of relaxation. Open your eyes. Move slightly. Start thinking again. This may take two or three minutes but you should emerge relaxed and with new energy.

354

The unnatural positions meditation – good for alertness at work

This is good for creating or maintaining alertness at work. Start by crossing your legs the way you always do. You will have either your right leg over your left or vice versa. Or, you will have your right ankle over your left, or vice versa.

Now, interlace your fingers. Your right thumb will be over your left thumb, your right index finger over your left, and so on, or vice versa.

Just sit there for about 60 seconds and enjoy how relaxing your habitual posture is, and how comfortable it makes you feel.

Now, cross your legs and interlace your fingers the opposite way. So, if you usually have your right foot crossed over your left and have your left thumb over your right, now put your left foot over your right and interlace all your fingers starting with your right thumb over your left. Now sit there for about 60 seconds.

Now you can pay attention. You will not be able to fall asleep even if you want to.

355

Sending positive energy to a loved one

* When you have established a steady, effortless, relaxed rhythm, focus your attention on your mind's eye.
* Receive love with every breath.
* Visualize love radiating from your heart to someone who needs love.
* See their heart fill with love, saturate every cell in their body, and radiate out from their heart in every direction.

356

Accept that all things are relative to each other

Where there is good, there is also evil.
Where there is beauty, there is also ugliness.
Where there is happiness, there is also sadness.
Where there is gain, there is also loss.

357

An exercise to increase awareness of your senses

❖ Relax your mind, body, and emotions.

❖ Breathe in and hold as long as is comfortable and exhale slowly and deeply. Breathing naturally, witness what your sense of smell is receiving now.

❖ Breathe in and hold as long as is comfortable and exhale slowly and deeply. Breathing naturally, witness what your sense of taste is receiving now.

❖ Breathe in and hold as long as is comfortable and exhale slowly and deeply. Breathing naturally, witness what your sense of hearing is receiving now.

❖ Breathe in and hold as long as is comfortable and exhale slowly and deeply. Breathing naturally, witness what your sense of sight is receiving now.

❖ Breathe in and hold as long as is comfortable and exhale slowly and deeply. Breathing naturally, witness what your mind is experiencing now.

✤ Inhale slowly and deeply. Hold as long as
   is comfortable and exhale slowly and
   deeply.
You should now be totally at peace with
yourself.

358

Meditation for forgiveness from others

As you enter your meditative state, think of
someone you've caused to suffer and send
them your healing, loving energy. Let them
realize they are receiving loving energy with
every inhalation and that they grow spiritually
to forgive you and all others who have harmed
them. And forever after, be free from guilt
about your transgression. You did not know
what you were doing then, and you would not
do it again now. With every breath, both be
forgiven and give forgiveness.

359

To free the mind, focus on something constant

The purpose of this meditation is to free the mind. No demands should be made on it by the external world or by your own directions or wishes.

The way to remove pressure from your mind is to focus your attention on one thing. This could be the flame of a candle, your own breathing or a simple pleasant sound (a mantra), such as "oohmm" or "hoomme", that you make each time you exhale.

Remember that you are giving up control to relaxation. The focusing should, with practice, become effortless and your mind will be able to float free.

360

To rid your mind of someone who is causing you unhappiness at the present time

Visualize a healing, loving, soothing light coming from every direction in the universe filling every cell in your body with a radiant glow. As your body gets brighter and brighter with light, an aura of healing, positive thought and goodness radiates out from your heart. In your mind's eye, as vividly as possible, see the person who is causing you the most pain right now. There are specific and general ways they have caused you pain. There is something within them that has caused them to act this way. In your mind, visualize it healing so that they may stop causing you this unhappiness.

361

Review the events of the day and resolve them before sleep

Every night before falling asleep, review the events of the day. Start with the first thing you remember and then continue in order as you remember them. Don't simply rehash how you usually go through your life's routine but rather note each nuance. An example would be if you dropped the bar of soap when you were washing your hands or heard alarming news over the radio while brushing your teeth. Try to recall how you reacted physically, mentally, and emotionally to every event of the day. If your reactions were bad ones, try to let go in your thoughts of these negative moments; if they were positive, take them as a true reflection of yourself. This will refresh you, ready for a new day tomorrow.

362

A Buddhist meditation technique for teaching appreciation of and compassion for others

This is an ancient Buddhist meditation technique which holds that compassion and humility are the two most important components of spiritual growth. It rests on the following thought.

Survival depends on the efforts of other people. Relax your mind, body, and emotions and contemplate all the ways in which you are dependent on others.

This meditation allows us to become warm toward others where previously we may not have cared.

363

When you meditate, you should pick a place which is as private and safe as possible. An altered state of mind, as in meditation, lessens your awareness of the outside world. If you are at home, with other family members or friends present, ask them not to disturb you and to keep all other noise in the house to a minimum. When you have found a place suitable for meditation, try to do your meditation in the same place every day.

364

Releasing sound and noise helps us release stress

Stand with your feet shoulder-width apart, your knees slightly bent and your hips centered, as though you're about to squat. If you wish, you can sit or lie down. Keep your body loose and comfortable, with your arms at your sides or on your hips. Begin by taking a few cleansing breaths. Next, pick a word. Choose a word that alternates vowels and consonants – like "serenity" or "happiness".

Repeat the word – chant it, over and over again. Let the sound of the word vibrate through your body. Let your muscles move as you chant the word. It is important to send the sound through your body so that you can clear out the tightness in your muscles.

365

Body meditation

✤ Lie on your back with your legs uncrossed,
  your arms at your sides, palms up, and
  your eyes open or closed, as you wish.

✤ Focus on your breathing and how the air
  moves in and out of your body.

✤ Pay particular attention to any areas that
  cause pain or are the focus of any medical
  condition. Then, pay particular attention
  to the head: the jaw, chin, lips, tongue,
  roof of the mouth, nostrils, throat, cheeks,
  eyelids, eyes, eyebrows, forehead, temples
  and scalp.

✤ Finally, focus on the very top of your hair,
  the uppermost part of your body. Then let
  go of the body altogether. By now your
  mind and body should be totally relaxed.